A LITTLE SAMMY MUSIC

Suzanne Lane

ISBN: 0692861467
ISBN 13: 9780692861462
Library of Congress Control Number: 2017904170
Suzanne Lane, New York, NY

DEDICATION

For Sammy.

Looking back it is unimaginable to recall a time when you weren't a part of my life. I am so grateful that somehow, against all odds, you found me.

And, for everyone who has the emotional capacity to pursue animal rescue as part, or all, of their daily lives, thank you. Without you, so many of us would never know the joy of sharing our lives with extraordinary four legged beings.

And, for Beatriz, Sandra, Harriet, Hedy and my dear Mother thank you from the depths of my heart.

Finally, for Mister, Tweety, Sebastian, Abbie and Astor. You each made my life sweeter, better and joyous!

All proceeds from the sale of this book will be donated to the animal rescue organization - 11th Hour Rescue.

PROLOGUE

These days, question marks walk with me all the time. Sometimes they grab my hand urgently, clamoring for attention, other times they merely trail behind me like gentle interlopers. They dance around in my head and whisper in my ears. Occasionally, they link an arm through mine, companionably, as if we're old friends. But, we're not.

These questions tug at the corners of my dreams. They have ripped open small seams of my life. They never go away. I have no answers, only more questions.

Yet, I have gotten ahead of myself, because in the beginning there were no questions, only doubts and misgivings.

CHAPTER 1

NEVER AGAIN!

I t would seem I am a born rescuer, though never by intent, always by accident and happenstance. Rarely do these rescues work out as I expect them to. I have rescued pigeons, dogs and cats, a fiancé, and one ex-husband. Some don't stay for long. Others do.

As a child, most of my rescues were culled from the street, like a little grey pigeon huddled under the canopy of the apartment building next to ours. This small bird presented myriad issues, among them was the fact that we had a dog, a Pekingese, named Mister. Mister might have been considered to be a rescue, but was in fact a prize, won after relentlessly badgering a colleague of my mother's, who had suddenly come into possession of a dog that she wasn't sure she wanted to keep. Mister's mission over the three days in which the bird stayed in our apartment, was to get the bird. This was not among my successes.

You might think I would have had a glimmer of an idea that rescuing was a dicey proposition, but I persevered and in my twenties rescued an orange fur ball of a tabby cat named Sebastian from a fiancé, named Bob. I had rescued Bob in a snowstorm by giving him a ride in my car, after he held up his thumb using the common gesture of hitchhikers, at a red light at which I had stopped;

so much for my parent's admonition about picking up hitchhikers. When it was clear the fiancé thing wasn't going to work, I snatched Sebastian, who lived out his life with me.

Later, as someone's wife, and after Sebastian died, I convinced my dubious husband that I couldn't live without an animal, and we wound up with two cats, Abigail and Astor, a brother and sister from Bide-a-Wee, a NYC shelter.

After Abbie, the last of the two, was diagnosed with bladder cancer, I was sure I had reached the end of my rescuing days. Abbie died at 17. My sweet little girl, who purred like an engine on steroids and never lost an opportunity to groom my face with her rough little tongue, poking her nose into my eyes and bumping my forehead, was tired. She was diagnosed a week before I put her to sleep. I could see her will and spirit slowly evaporate and I knew that kindness could only be delivered by doing something that even now brings me terrible pain. I mourned her loss with an intensity that seared me. And, when I said "Never again," I meant it. The pain was too extraordinary. My rescuing days were officially over.

Astor, and later, Abbie were buried in a pet cemetery that was Sebastian's resting place. Nestled in a swath of land cut into the middle of a forest in Montgomery, NY, Abbingdon Hill is as close to the perfect cemetery as one can get, if, indeed, there is such a thing. Grave stones are set randomly throughout the property looking like part of the landscape. The headstones with their carefully chosen sentiments spoke of such tenderness and love that tears for animals I never knew came easily here.

But, what makes Abbingdon Hill truly remarkable is the group of cats and dogs who are tended to by the staff and who freely wander the cemetery, attaching themselves to each newcomer as if by appointment. When my ex-husband and I buried Sebastian we were met at the car door by a pure white cat, who stayed with us until we left. We never glimpsed the orange tabby we were told was part of this pack. How unusual for him to stay hidden the undertaker mused.

When Astor died, I vowed to bring Abbie back to him one day and made sure that when the time came, they could be buried together in the same grave.

CHAPTER 2

THE MORE THINGS CHANGE . . . .

In the two years after Abbie died, I somehow expected my life to change. My brief stint with online dating, after my divorce, abandoned while the cats were alive and almost always sick, had not entirely soured me. So, I began in earnest looking for a human companion. I can't say I met with resounding success. It was really difficult. The men who contacted me seemed to be looking for more or less what could be found in a bar at closing time, while the men I contacted were not interested. I couldn't figure out the formula.

One reality of online dating became very evident; the fact that I was a business owner, and an apartment owner, weighed heavily against me. And, online, as in real life, first impressions are first impressions and nothing I could do with the exception of making up a new life for myself would change the reality.

So, I continued, expecting each time, it would be different; and in truth, it was, different each time, that is. The men were so strange in person. One was difficult to speak to on the phone as he grunted, panted and heaved into the receiver. What he was doing, as he moaned, was very clear. Another moved from apartment to apartment every year, never really unpacking his belongings. "What is that about?" I wondered.

Finally, I settled on an off line, in person, very sexy, Italian man who owned a business in my neighborhood. I had happened to walk in to buy a picture frame and I was quite unexpectedly charmed by an accent and a pair of dark brown eyes that bored into me. Chemistry, wow! I had forgotten what it felt like. He offered, yes I know how absurd this is, to deliver the picture frame. I said yes. It seemed we had some sort of ill-defined date?

I prepared fruit and cheese. He wore a freshly laundered shirt that smelled very subtly of starch, my favorite male scent. We sat on my sofa and talked for hours and at some point I had a realization.

"Are you married?" I asked. "Mezza, mezza," he responded. How can one be married "half and half?" I asked. Did it matter to me? Not really. I wasn't looking for permanence I realized, just company and he was that! And, he continued to be that for several years. I didn't need more.

I think this requires a word about only children, which I am . . . . Some of us need to be surrounded by people, others not so much. I was in the not so much camp. Going out, just to be out, didn't do it for me. My occupation is public relations. It requires being "on," a lot. Sometimes I yearned for quiet. No phones, no talk, just quiet and a cozy animal, or it seems a married man, to cuddle up with. But, the cozy animal wasn't part of my life any longer.

So I set up little personal challenges for myself. Things I could do on my own without making excuses. There was no man in my life, so why pretend otherwise. I stopped ordering two different entrees when I called for Chinese take-out! I didn't slip my old wedding ring on when shopping for clothes, feeling pathetic if it was after five on a Saturday night. My biggest challenge was going to a movie alone. I tried a few times, but chickened out. Then, finally, I worked up my courage, ordered one ticket online and actually went in. I sat on an aisle seat, bought popcorn and a Diet Coke. I looked around, but found no one staring at me in pity. The lights dimmed and wonder of wonders, I loved being alone. It became a routine activity. But, still something in my life felt lopsided.

And, then came the craving. I imagine it might be a little of what an addict feels when there are no drugs. At about the two year mark I started gazing with longing at every dog on the street. And, when we passed each other I would turn around to see that many of the dogs had turned around too, looking back at me with what seemed to be recognition of some sort. I could feel the longing become a physical thing. I needed a dog. I mentioned this to no one, for I feared the chorus of "You must be crazy to do this again," echoing from every person who knew me well.

CHAPTER 3

THIS DOG WILL DIE

I was working from home on my computer one day when I read an email from a former classmate of mine from high school. Her email was short, cryptic and heartbreaking. Alongside a picture of a terribly sad looking dog with his head bowed, was the message. "This dog will die tomorrow if someone doesn't get him out of the system." "What do you mean?" I wrote back.

"He will be euthanized tomorrow morning if someone doesn't get him," she responded and without thinking for even a second, I replied, "I'll take him!" I had no idea what breed he was, how big he was, only that his head seemed enormous and his eyes were defeated.

My former classmate told me to get in touch with someone named Harriet and make arrangements. I did and was amazed at the paperwork involved in saying "I'll take him." It seemed I was adopting a child. Page after page needed to be filled out and after a week, during which I found out my new dog was living in the unheated basement of a foster family, he was ready to be delivered from Brooklyn.

I prepared for the arrival by buying stuffed dog toys and ordering chicken soup with half a chicken. I'm Jewish and it appears to run in the blood.

And then they arrived. Harriet was a lovely and thankful middle-aged woman with grey-tinged, brown hair and, the being, who would be named Sammy, looking like a weary voyager, was astounding to behold, more like a snow leopard than a dog. Black and white smudges, big black ears and soulful eyes, he didn't look like any dog I had ever seen.

"I do Dalmatian rescue," Harried hurriedly explained as she saw me appraise this solemn, distinctly not-a-Dalmatian dog. "And when the shelter told me they had one I went to get him. I knew he wasn't a Dalmatian the moment I saw him, but he needed to be taken away from that awful place." There was a silent plea in her eyes.

I wasn't listening though, because as I sat on the floor, the one who would be called Sammy, leaned all his weight into me and I did something so primal. I smelled him. Right next to his right ear and his smell pleased me. It registered in a place I didn't know I had and can't really explain. I hugged him because he seemed so desperately in need of hugging. He sighed. Harriet smiled.

But, we had only just begun our first night's odyssey. Harriet checked everything in my apartment, the furniture, the doors, the windows. She asked me dozens of questions. I just nodded. "They called him Spot at the shelter," she explained, "so I wouldn't try to change his name yet. If you want to call him something else, attach it to Spot."

I did want to call him something else. Sammy. I wanted to name him in the memory of Samantha, a cocker spaniel who had been the love of one of my clients and his wife. Steve and Paula became Sammy's godparents, albeit in Texas.

I got to know very little about Sammy from Harriet or the intake sheets from the shelter. His age, for one thing was a puzzle;

somewhere between three and seven. It wasn't until several years later and by accident that I learned he was five when he came to me. In fact, he had just turned five. Where he had lived was a mystery. Everything seemed to be a mystery. The shelter gave me little information, they gave Sammy a neutering and a chip to identify him and we were off and running.

What I did learn was that the shelter had a "three strikes and you're out policy." Sammy had been adopted by a family, who upon determining that he wasn't well, he had kennel cough, promptly returned him. Another family with a cat, upon being reassured that Sammy would not hurt their cat – the shelter assured them based upon placing a cat in a carrier in a room and introducing Sammy into the room. When both animals, probably already traumatized, did nothing, they assumed he was good with cats. Sammy, on the other hand, when arriving in their home and seeing a real live cat, began the chase. And with that began his journey back to the shelter. Turns out they had a two strikes and you're out policy!

Harriet delivered Sammy in a beat up looking black woolen horse-blanket type winter coat with a big bag of IAMs lamb flavored dry food. He also came with packets of a white powder called Panacur, for some kind of parasite, but Harriet didn't know the exact name. She had taken him to a vet, not my former clinic, which gave people like me with, what I now understood were called, "rescue dogs," a discount.

She also delivered the news that the vet was pretty sure Sammy was part Pit Bull. All I knew about Pits back then was that they were not to be trusted. But, this sad looking creature, who followed me everywhere, looked about as ferocious as a pillow. On the street, however, as Harriet accompanied us on our first official walk, he barked at every dog, walked into the headlights of cars waiting at red lights and wanted to climb every set of brownstone steps he saw. Harriet assured me that he just needed to get used to his new environment and she left. And in that moment, Sammy and I began our life together.

I thought having had a dog, the instincts of knowing what to do would come back easily; like riding a bike. They did not. I used to have neighbors who had a Schnauzer named Fred, who I walked periodically. But Fred was 25 pounds and accustomed to NYC streets. Sammy, it seemed, was not. I was more than clueless. Our walks were erratic, without a destination and very, very long. I got to know a lot of the doormen on West End Avenue, who smiled as they saw me zig zagging down the street behind my dog. My dog!

On the day after Sammy arrived I had taken him to get a new coat. He was short haired with thick, bristly fur, but his ratty, old coat was covered in all kinds of dog hair and Harriet asked that I mail it back to the foster home, so it could keep a future rescue warm.

I decided he needed not only a new winter coat, but a rain coat and a new harness and leash. He needed to be measured for these and getting him to stand still in the pet store was completely impossible. He was so excited by all the things he saw at eye level and higher, he went bouncing from one aisle to another while the sales clerk followed behind with a tape measure. "Is he always like this?" he asked, amused and exasperated. I had no idea.

CHAPTER 4

BIG DOGS ARE DIFFERENT

Let me just say that big dogs are different than little ones. Not to state the obvious, but they are so different. As our vet nurse, Sandra, is fond of saying, "Their junk is bigger!" It certainly is. And, Sammy loved to spend time lying on his back, displaying his to anyone and everyone, hoping for the much desired belly rub.

Big dogs also take up much more space.

The first night we spent together, Sammy jumped on my king sized bed and proceeded to occupy it. Stretched out he seemed to be about four feet long from his head to the tip of his tail. He apparently liked to sleep horizontally at the foot of the bed. I tucked myself in next to his head and we slept until three in the morning, when all at once and out of a deep sleep, this new bedmate of mine leaped into the air and charged at the front door of the apartment, a distance of at least 60 feet from the bedroom.

He barked because a neighbor was entering the apartment next to mine and his door had slammed. I was in trouble, I thought, as I urged him back to the bedroom. Was he, in fact, a fearsome Pit Bull, I wondered? We went back to bed and I closed the door. How else to curtail this nocturnal activity and not incur my co-op board's inevitable wrath?

At this point, may I just say, Oy!!!!!

The next morning found my new dog pooping in the living room, urinating on every available anything and needing to go out 14 times. On the 14th walk, I came out of the elevator in tears. Upon seeing me yet again, my doorman took the leash, told me to watch the door and he made the 14th walk. Oh my God was I in trouble!!!!!!

CHAPTER 5

NEVER SAY "NO"

Anyone who gets a new dog also gets plenty of advice from everyone. Not all of it is good and there is no "one rule fits all" policy. Like humans, dogs are individuals. My new individual knew a prime pee spot when he saw one; whether it was the plastic dry cleaning bag or the corner of my bed. God, could this dog pee!!!!! But, he was very smart. When I screeched "No!" at him, he stopped, in the moment . . . only to find a new spot a little later.

"Don't say no to him," offered some well-intentioned souls, probably the same people who had been taught to never say no to their children; an idiotic concept that I have never understood. What on earth is wrong with saying no? I should give my dog a distraction the "no-no-sayers," said.

"A distraction?" I asked, astonished by the stupidity of this idea. "Here sweetheart, don't pee there, pee here?" I didn't think so. I did, however. hang his leash on the front door and Sammy quickly learned if he needed to go out he went to his leash. I think, truthfully, he played me a little with this, loving to go out and explore. He did, and everyone who has known Sammy agrees, have an enormous well of urine with which to mark his territory, both outdoors and in. The indoor marking continued, but we only walked nine times the second day and only seven times on day three. The same day that, in his haste to smell something on the street, I lost my footing, went down on one knee, ripped my pants and bled, a lot.

After the first two weeks, one of my neighbors, seeing my out of control and seemingly endless walks, offered me a helpful piece of advice. She fished around in her handbag for a pen and a piece of paper. What was she doing I wondered as she carefully wrote down the telephone number of her dog walker. "Her name is Ellen," my neighbor told me and you will love her. She's great with our dog." Their dog was a large Labradoodle and I thought if Ellen could manage Kirby, she might have a chance with Sammy.

So, Ellen and her dog, Mugsy, arrived in our lives. Ellen was wise and calm and proceeded to educate me. She sat on the floor in my foyer and recited a list of helpful tidbits of information. She was used to these first meetings with novice dog people. Mugsy, in the meantime, took off down the long hall of the apartment, dodging in and out of rooms. "She was a real estate broker in a former life," Ellen confided. "She's measuring the space."

Mugsy and Sammy fell instantly in love, a euphoric, giddy at the sight of one another, love that has endured through the years. An alpha female, with a rich black coat and a bark of immense authority, she would crawl backwards on a wall on the street to mark over Sammy's pee. She owned him, ruled him and he adored her. Feisty, part Border collie, Mugsy had him by his, no longer, balls.

Mugsy and Sammy had dates, because Sammy needed to be better socialized, advised Ellen. So, on many Sunday mornings she and I would eat brunch in my living room while the two dogs cavorted, until the day Mugsy realized there was Nova Scotia salmon on the dining room table. "She loves salmon," said Ellen, "but, only if it comes from Zabar's." This renowned gourmet store had many varieties of smoked salmon, but Mugsy's choice was always Scotch-cured and she could easily eat a half a pound and beg for more. Our brunches turned into a costly affair. But watching the two dogs interact made it worthwhile. At least in this respect I was enjoying my dog.

I also enjoyed watching Sammy with Ellen. Not an openly demonstrative woman, she nevertheless had Sammy's attention from day one. As much as he was charmed by Mugsy, he also devoted time to Ellen, coming to her repeatedly to be stroked and acknowledged. On the street, if we ran into them unexpectedly, Sammy expressed boundless joy at the sight of Mugsy, but also came to Ellen to say hello. If he couldn't get her attention, in a rare move for Sammy, he got up on his hind legs and put his paws on her chest. He wanted her to say hello back and would pull out his entire repertoire of "look at me" moves to gain her attention. A sometimes distracted individual, Ellen would speak to Sammy when he did this, but always with a semi "somewhere else" affect. In a few minutes Sammy would abandon this pursuit and turn back to Mugsy who was always available for a romp and a sniff.

Tangled up in leashes, if we met on the street, this interaction between them was one that didn't frighten me, because I knew that if Mugsy needed to reprimand Sammy, she could be counted on to do it in a way that wouldn't scare him. Tangled up in leashes with other dogs basically unhinged me as there was too little wiggle room in the mess of leashes to intervene if the interaction looked as if it was going bad. I wasn't very adept at reading the moves that dogs use to signal playfulness to other dogs and I marveled at the calm with which other dog owners allowed their dogs to become intertwined amidst a lot of jumping up and down and growling.

CHAPTER 6

PAY ATTENTION TO YOUR INSTINCTS

Easing into life with a dog, and having finished the Panacur, I did think Sammy's breathing wasn't quite right. He would wake up with labored panting. At first I thought maybe it was stress, but instinctively I knew it was more. So we trotted off to the new vet. It was a big step down from the veterinary hospital to which I had taken Abbie and Astor. The vet, a man in his mid-fifties, gaunt and serious, examined Sammy and told me he was fine, just residual coughing from kennel cough.

In the next moment I began my first step of advocacy for this being who was in my charge. I argued for a chest x-ray and finally after insisting I would pay full price, the vet discovered that Sammy was close to developing pneumonia. "Good catch," the vet said. "Screw you," I wanted to say, but didn't. We went home with piles of antibiotics.

Next, came the scooting. Sammy would drop his butt to the floor and drag himself around. It looked painful and off to the same vet we went. Anal gland infection was the diagnosis. More antibiotics. And, through every visit, Sammy was amazing and compliant, perhaps grateful in his own way to know he was being cared for.

Of all the people who had a lot to say and not very kindly, about this new addition to my life, the chorus of "how could you?" "what were you thinking," "more pain," "you aren't cut out for this," my mother stood as the lone voice of dissent.

At 92, she said, "I am glad you have him. You will need him." Sammy fell in love with my mother and she with him. I didn't know what she meant by "you will need him," but I guessed. He would visit with her, sat close to her on the couch and for someone with zero experience with a large dog, my mother was a pro.

She lived in an assisted living residence on West End Avenue and every time we visited she would ask me, "Do you love him?" And I would truthfully answer "No." Sammy was a lot of work. I never expected how much. He still wasn't house trained. The pooping indoors had stopped, but every time I turned around it seemed he was about to raise his leg on something.

Left to my own devices with this situation I created a solution. He was too old to be crated and I thought it would remind him of the shelter. So, instead I gave him my guest room. I thought, perhaps in the room, he would learn to respect his new home. I was basically flying by the seat of my pants in unchartered territory with a housemate I hadn't been prepared for.

Every day we would wake up, wait for Ellen and Mugsy and then Sammy had breakfast . . . and tried also to have mine, along with anything worthwhile in the garbage. There was no peace until mid-morning when I would put him in the guest room with a fresh bowl of water, some toys and a huge round, brown velveteen dog bed that he tried exuberantly to tear into bits. I would leave his leash on the door handle, exiting with a false sounding round of "have a good day sweetie, Barry will be here soon." Barry was the two o'clock walker. And only then would I exhale and get ready for work.

In the evening, I would arrive at my front door, plaster a fake smile on my lips and go into the apartment and open the guest room door to find my roomie on the other side so happy to be re-leased from confinement. I would make dinner, give him his bowl in the kitchen and then take a tray into my bedroom. He followed. He climbed on to my lap and tried to eat my dinner. If he left me alone I would often find him routing around in the garbage can. A loud and very frequent round of the forbidden word, "No," was always on my lips.

One night I discovered him with the overturned garbage pail, eating shrimp shells and leftover cucumber salad. He could not be left alone. He may have learned to scrounge for food on the street. I never learned if he did live on the street for a while before arriving at the shelter, but the fact that I eventually found his birth date in the intake papers belied the idea of his having been a street dog. When he arrived at my front door he weighed 42.7 pounds. He needed to acquire weight, the vet advised and Sammy began to gain weight immediately, so it wasn't that he wasn't get enough to eat. He just wouldn't stop.

At times though, I caught possible glimpses of Sammy's for-mer life. Like the time I screamed "No," and threw my hands up in the air in exasperation. He cowered. My heart heaved at my mistake. Perhaps he had been beaten. He had a horseshoe shaped scar above his left eye. I never raised my hand again. But, I wasn't having a good time.

A neighbor of mine met us in the park one day with his black lab, Sadie.

"Hey, Sammy from Miami," he called. To me he said, "Isn't hav-ing a dog in your life such a joyous experience?"

I must have looked blank. "Really?" I thought. "What part of this is joyous? When does joyous begin?" It was winter and very cold and our nighttime walks, in particular, were at least a mile in duration and I didn't own a hat or a winter jacket with a hood. I was so ill-equipped both mentally and physically.

And then, finally, I was exhausted. Left with no recourse, I began the laborious task of finding a new home for Sammy. I asked two women, both with dogs, in the park, huddled together in the freezing January early morning cold. Did either one want this dog of mine? One, who did animal rescue, told me to have patience.

"Rescue dogs come with a history," she explained. "It may take time." She invited us over for a "play date." It didn't get better. The dogs ran around and cavorted all over her apartment. Sammy was awkward in this activity. He was eager to follow, but didn't seem to know what to do. This wasn't like playing with Mugsy I thought.

"He doesn't know how to do this very well," I said to our host, who was so amazingly relaxed. How did one achieve this state of Zen, I wondered. Sammy couldn't find the natural rhythm the other two dogs seemed to have with one another. He ran happily behind them, but they didn't pay much attention to his inept attempts to interject himself in their play. Everything seemed so new to him.

CHAPTER 7

FROM BAD TO WORSE

The things no one prepared me for:

Sammy chased squirrels
Sammy was totally untrained
Sammy ate other dog's poop

And, in his quest to eat poop, Sammy got into a shitload of trouble.

Let's begin with the squirrels. Had I been prepared I might have known which way to turn the first time my dog spotted a squirrel in the park and almost dislocated my shoulder. He lunged so hard and with such force, my arm went momentarily numb. He bellowed at the squirrel and tried to chase it up a tree with me flying behind him. Thank God squirrels move fast. I too, learned fast. I was on my guard when we approached a group of pigeons, but it seemed pigeons were largely exempt. Rats, not so much.

I had no idea how many rats lived in my neighborhood or that late at night on Manhattan's pricey upper west side, rats ruled the wee hours. And, they were big. I am not afraid of rats, oddly, but Sammy was obsessed. He looked under cars, in basement court-yards, anywhere he had seen something scurry through the streets.

His eyesight was keen. My arms hurt from the strain. Worse yet, he remembered, from walk to walk, exactly where he had sighted his prey. He prowled the streets, looking.

My screaming "no," wasn't doing an enormous amount of good. Yes, he was peeing less frequently in the house, but he strained at his leash and was a general maniac on the street. It would have been comical had it not been so fatiguing. I had no idea what had possessed me to adopt him, for adopting is what I did. His chip now bore my name and address. He was, lock, stock and barrel, registered to me.

CHAPTER 8

GET A TRAINER

"Get a trainer," a few people told me. So, I hired a trainer. I didn't much like the trainer. He used his knee to keep Sammy close to the walls of buildings and to stop him from criss-crossing in front of him as was Sammy's wont. After all, if something smelled good on one side of the street, might not there be something of equal or greater value on the other side? I secretly thought it was funny. Very hound-like. But, not when it went on for block after block every time we walked together. My 2 PM walker, Barry, quit. "He's too strong and big for me to handle," he said sadly. "But, don't worry there are a lot of good, younger walkers." And, I went through them like candy. They came in all sizes, sexes, shapes and ages.

"Eventually," the trainer I didn't like, told me, "You will be able to say 'poop,' and he will on command." Not this dog," I thought. He will never do anything on command. I didn't call the trainer to come back.

I was so unprepared for this next chapter in our lives. We were out walking around 11 at night and as was my way until then, I didn't spend a lot of time inspecting the street for what might be hidden anywhere. So, when Sammy lunged for something and came up with his mouth askew, I suspected there was something inside. I reached a finger in his mouth and sure enough there was a cigar. Or so I thought, until I smelled my finger! There really are no words to describe this adequately. Disgust, of course. Horror, that my dog had tried to scarf down a piece of dog poop. Yes. But, what would I do about it? I was lost.

Sprinkle some Accent in his food, someone counseled me. But it turns out this only works for dogs who try to eat their own poop. "When he tries, squirt Binaca in his mouth," said a neighborhood dog walker who I knew. "Squirt lemon in his mouth," said another. "Dogs hate citrus." But, what I quickly learned was that Accent, Binaca and lemons had no power over my dog. What these all did was conspire to make him try harder. My dog was defiant! Binaca indeed, I could hear his dog voice in my head. Really???

Then, one night on our late walk I ran into an old classmate on west 86th street with her little rescue dog, a white shaggy somewhat disheveled dog. While we chatted, she eyed Sammy and casually said to me, "Look at what your dog is doing."

I turned to discover Sammy, snout deep in a black garbage bag inside a hole he had apparently chewed open. When I pulled out his head, his mouth was overflowing with what smelled like some sort of Chinese cabbage. I took fistfalls of this cabbage out of his mouth much to his dismay. My classmate chortled and leaving her in the middle of a loud guffaw, we took off. I was overcome with exhaustion. He required such vigilance.

As we rounded the corner heading back home, he managed to snag a piece of poop!!! It was too much! I opened his mouth, because oddly I never had any fear of Sammy, and I shook his head to dislodge the excrement. Two older women, walking arm in arm towards us watched and as I struggled to keep the poop from going down his throat, one said to the other in not much of a whisper, "Honestly, some people just shouldn't have dogs." I thought that sadly, perhaps she was right.

I tried to persevere though, encouraged by my mother and my vet. I got the name of a renowned behaviorist, a man in his sixties, who showed up at my apartment one evening. Tall, broad shouldered and with a lovely smile, I thought maybe he had an answer.

He proceeded to spend two hours fashioning a loop to fit around Sammy's snout and proclaimed that my dog, my dog who dragged me for at least 15 city blocks at each walk, wasn't getting enough "sniff time." This is absurd, I thought. All he does is sniff. But, I dutifully went out and bought what he recommended, a retractable leash that expanded out to 30 feet. "Take him to a dog run," proclaimed this well-known expert, "let him socialize more."

So I did what he told me to do. I bought the leash and had less control than ever and I took Sammy to the dog park, where I soon learned he had no desire to socialize with other dogs and truthfully, the place was scary. Dogs of all sizes were barreling back and forth and the sounds they made as they tumbled over each other didn't sound all that friendly. Maybe I just didn't get it, I mused and looked around to find Sammy.

He, as it turned out loved the dog park. The perimeter that is. Because, there, unfettered by a leash, he was able to eat other dog's poop to his heart's content.

CHAPTER 9

I WAS NOT PREPARED

It began that evening. My dog who usually produced perfectly shaped poop, tried to squat, then got up, tried to squat again and finally produced a flood of diarrhea. The dog park I thought. The God damn dog park. I remember Ellen, my dog walker telling me that canned pumpkin was a good way to stop diarrhea. I ran out and bought two giant cans. It worked. Sort of.

But, Sammy didn't look well. I didn't lock him in the guest room because I was afraid he was sick, but for the next few days we were on a roller coaster of sorts. One good day, one bad.

I called the vet. "Give him boiled chicken and rice," they counseled. I did. We went to the park for a walk and he had what can only be described as diarrhea water. I was scared. I called the vet. They persisted with the chicken and rice counsel, but that night Sammy vomited the chicken and leaned against me, wasted and tired and so sick. I called the vet and got their answering machine. Finally, the vet's estranged wife, also a vet, called me back and told me to bring him in first thing in the morning.

Somehow we got there, and he seemed better, but we were not taken right away, so I walked Sammy a bit in Central Park, where he promptly leaked out more watery diarrhea and in one of my first instinctive moves, because the vet had not asked for this, I grabbed a clump of diarrhea soaked leaves in a baggie and took it back to the vet. To her credit the ex-wife partner examined what I brought her under a microscope and pronounced that she found giardia.

I had no idea what that meant. It meant she explained that Sammy was full of a parasite that had colonized his intestines, making him very sick. She gave me medicine, something called Flagyl and sent us home. But Sammy was even sicker that night and I was scheduled to fly to San Francisco the next day. The plan had been that Ellen and Mugsy were going to stay in my apartment for the five days I would be gone, but now everything was in the air.

I called the vet pleading for help for this very sick dog and the female partner told me to get him in a taxi and come over. He would be admitted. It was frigid outside with snow hanging in the air when we piled into a taxi which stopped for us after many had passed refusing to stop for a big dog. I offered the driver twenty dollars for a five block trip and we landed at the vet's door. Not at all like the old veterinary clinic that had 24 hour care with a nurse on duty overnight and a doctor on call, this place had one long, cold room with kennels piled on top of each other and one long caged in run. The only other occupant was a cat. I felt bad, but didn't know what else to do and I left him. It seemed like a plan because at the very least he would be monitored. However, with no overnight staff, there was no monitoring.

I called Ellen, briefed her on everything and we agreed she would check in with the vet along with me, albeit long distance. I felt uncomfortable, but he was sick and I couldn't come up with a better plan.

Why, you may be wondering, hadn't I gone back to my old vet? It's a long story, not worth telling, but it came down to an extremely condescending attitude – his, and an "I am not taking this anymore" attitude – mine. At the end of Abbie's life he had screamed at me when I asked for a consult with a feline urologist and when everything was over I had no intention of ever seeing him again.

One could argue that I was attached to Sammy by this point because I was doing everything in my power to help him. But, the love, the joy were absent. I was doing all the right things out of obligation, but feeling more and more helpless. I even asked Ellen if she thought he would remember me when I came back from California. "Are you kidding?" she asked, "Of course he will remember you."

As this saga played out, I left for California with Ellen promising to check in with Sammy's vet every day. I was worried, but somehow detached. That changed when Ellen called me two days later to say she had taken Sammy out of the vet's office because she could give him pills as well at home and why should he have to stay in this "miserable" place. I was so relieved, not realizing I had been very anxious. Was it love? No. But, it was concern.

I should interrupt myself at this point to say that on one of my Sammy walks I had run into a nurse from my old vet's office. So surprised to see me walking a dog after my cat history, she asked why I hadn't come back to the clinic with Sammy. I told her how I felt about my old vet and she promptly countered with "Well, you haven't met Dr. Downy yet." I looked skeptical. She didn't stop. "She's amazing," she raved. "You would love her." I parked that piece of information away and proceeded to forget it, but remembered while I was in San Francisco.

When I came home I was delighted to find Sammy and Mugsy racing down the hall to meet me. Honestly, I was surprised. We walked Ellen and Mugsy home to her building and came home where I gave Sammy a new toy I had bought for him. My dog, the "Eviscerator," as I began to think of him because he found every hidden seam in every toy and destroyed it with stuffing flying everywhere, ripped the toy from my hands and ran down the hall.

A moment later I heard him scream. I flew out of my bedroom to find him collapsed on the floor, whimpering. As best as I can tell, in his haste to run down the long hallway apparently he caught his leg in the French door dissecting the path and while most of him went forward, his left hind leg didn't. When he got up, he could barely walk. Now, I wondered, where was I going to take him to be repaired? I swallowed my angst at returning to the old vet's clinic. It was two blocks away and I thought we could hobble the distance.

CHAPTER 10

SAMMY AND THE NEW VET

My childhood dog, Mister, would never go anywhere near his vet's office, but Sammy was overflowing with joy at meeting anyone, anywhere. Endearing as it was, here we were at a vet's office again, now the fourth time in three months, albeit in clean new surroundings.

True to her description, Dr. Downy was amazing. Kind hearted and sweet she greeted Sammy with tenderness and praise for his unique looks. He ate it up. Yes, as it turned out whenever we went to the vet he was overjoyed . . . . because he got enormous adulation and treats. It was all about the treats and as ebullient as he was, he was also rambunctious, standing on his hind legs, pushing the examination stool out of the way to try to reach the cookie jars that were in every exam room. Even with a limp.

He was charming, I thought, as he barked his entrance to anyone who would listen. Had he arrived in a black cape and top hat, it would not have surprised me. "Tah dah," was his arrival theme just about everywhere. For clients sitting in the waiting room with very sick animals however, it was not so endearing and I had zero control. I apologized to anyone who looked annoyed, because truly there was nothing I could do. Eventually, whenever we arrived at the vet's, the reception staff didn't even look up. "It's Sammy," they would say. I was embarrassed, but secretly amused. They fawned over him. He was so unlike any dog that anyone, apparently, had ever seen.

So in about four days Sammy's leg healed, but the twisting of limbs became fairly routine. "Clumsy," Dr. Downy diagnosed fondly. "Sammy is a very clumsy dog." He was also, as it turned out, very prone to giardia infections and because I wasn't present on every walk, I don't know how carefully he was watched as he could snag a piece of poop with such stealth he was very hard to monitor. I stopped looking up while walking him, eyes trained ten steps ahead scouring the pavement for anything that might be edible.

I began looking longingly at firm dog poop on the street, waiting for the day that Sammy's would look normal again, not like a pile of mush. It was a very long wait. I kept my eyes peeled for a new family for him. It was so overwhelming.

CHAPTER 11

WHAT TO DO?

I asked just about every reasonable person I knew or almost knew if they would take my dog. My housekeeper, Beatriz, volunteered to try. She had a very large black lab named Mike, who thundered out of our elevator for a "play date," wearing an enormous choke collar and looking like Zeus.

Sammy, waiting, as he liked to do for every new arrival, was in the hall off leash. When they saw each other for the first time, Mike and Sammy's barking, was a cacophony of howls and ferocious barks. I immediately herded Sammy into my apartment and put his leash on, but it was clear, this was not a match made in heaven. It wouldn't work. Mike had at least forty pounds on Sammy, who had blossomed to 60 pounds from his scrawny arrival day. Fully muscled and firm, he was such a handsome dog. "Truly righteous," a man declared upon seeing him in the park one day. "That is a righteous looking dog." And he was, but no match for Mike, whose body rippled with strength.

I asked a doorman in the neighborhood who told me he had a pit bull named Tank, who resembled Sammy, if he would take Sammy. They seemed to like each other so much. He hesitated and said to come back if I couldn't find anyone. A twenty-something man walking with a group of friends on Broadway called to me one evening, "That's an amazing looking dog." "Do you want him?" I asked. "Are you serious?" he replied. I handed the leash to him, but immediately withdrew it. Are you insane I asked myself? Who is this guy? You can't simply give Sammy away and not know to whom. But, I was undaunted.

I called the rescue lady, Harriet and asked her if she could find him a new home. She sighed. "I thought he would be a Cinderella story," she said sadly. "Would you foster him while I search for a new home for him?" I agreed.

One night on our walk a family of a husband, wife and little girl encountered us on the street. The girl flung her arms around Sammy and he licked her face. Unusual for him. "Were they looking for a dog," I inquired. The woman said they had been considering it and looked at her husband. "Oh please Daddy, please," pined the girl. We stood and talked as the husband put packages away in the trunk of their car, not looking all that enthusiastic. They lived in a house in Connecticut. Yes, they had a fenced in backyard. I told them I was fostering Sammy. Didn't mention the giardia, thinking I could confess all later, and gave them my contact information. But they never called.

And then came the by then routine question from my mother "So, do you love him a little?" she questioned while petting him with one gnarled, arthritic hand. I admitted it just wasn't happening. He had so many issues.

My mother by then had advanced macular degeneration and dropped her medication everywhere. So whenever we visited I did a quick site inspection to make sure nothing was on the floor. But, that day I missed something.

The next moment I saw Sammy scoop it off the floor and crunch. I pried open his mouth to see something that looked like a crushed white pill go down his throat. My mother took several different kinds of pills, one for blood pressure, another to thin her blood, vitamins for her eye, laxatives. I grabbed the phone and called the vet. I told her what happened and she wrote down all the names of the pills. "Bring him in," she said. "We need to do blood work."

He needed to stay for three days. I used the time to desperately find him a new place to live. I tried humane shelters, but they wouldn't take a dog with giardia. No one would take him in. And then it hit me. Could I really give him away? I spent the three days in tears torn between the reality of a beautiful, sweet, poop eating, clumsy, rambunctious dog and the idea of living with guilt. For though we hadn't bonded, there was nevertheless a bond between this crazy dog and me.

In that time I was also struck by a thought, that for someone like me who is absolutely not religious and only amused, but not convinced, by anything metaphysical, that the reason Sammy wouldn't leave was not because I couldn't find him a home, but because he was meant to stay. Being science-minded, I reasoned that if energy never died, perhaps one of my failed rescues' energy was in Sammy and it was determined to live out its life with me through my dog. As strange as the idea was it stuck. It sticks to this day.

His toxicology screen came back clean and there was no evidence of damage, so Sammy was cleared to come home. By now, with all the false positive giardia tests, all the twisted ankles and knees, Sammy's chart looked like that of a twelve year old dog, not a five year old one. I had only had him for five months.

And here he came again, clambering down the stairs from his confinement on the second floor. He spotted me from the staircase and raced towards me with the nurse flying behind him and threw himself into my lap.

What happened next I can't really explain, because who can ever really explain matters of the heart? It was very simple, one moment I was consumed by dread and the next moment I was deep in love. I absolutely and completely fell in love with this crazy black and white maniac. The love was so overwhelming that I began to cry. I showered him with kisses. Standing up on his hind legs, front legs in my lap, he gazed at me quizzically. I imagine he wondered, " Who is this woman?" We headed home as if for the first time.

The funny thing is that as my heart opened wide to let him in, he changed too, maybe sensing what had been missing up until then. He loved me back. It was joyous. I understood my neighbor in the park. It was a magnificent feeling. I loved Sammy. I called my mother.

CHAPTER 12

CAN OPENERS???

In the days after Sammy came fully into my heart I mused about the event that caused this to happen, for it was very sudden. It occurred to me that dogs and cats are a little bit like nature's can openers for some of us. They open the lids of our closed jars allowing in a very special kind of love.

For some the lid is closed tight because they have never known the love of an animal. For others, and I was beginning to see myself as one of these types, the lid of the jar is tightly screwed on, because we have experienced this kind of profound love and the terrible sorrow that always awaits us at the end. I tried in vain to avoid that feeling again and in retrospect, while Sammy was difficult, it was my paralyzing fear of plunging in again that had denied me the joy of him. For joy it was, unquestionably. I was no match for this sweet, gentle soul who charmed so many people.

As I grew to understand him, I realized that Sammy was an extremely social being, who would not tolerate being ignored. He tamed me and trained me and tried to do the same with total strangers. In later years, when my mother needed a full time companion and I interviewed one after another looking for a match, we met a timid, middle-aged black woman, who spoke with a

Caribbean accent and always clutched her handbag to her chest. She was terrified of Sammy, but I wasn't about to leave him at home when visiting my mother, denying her the pleasure of spending time with him, and him with her.

This woman, who radiated fear, and ennui simultaneously, and who largely ignored my mother, sat on my mother's couch one day, as my mother lay in her bed in the other room. Sammy, determined to get her to acknowledge him, finally, jumped up on the other end of the couch and quietly lay down. "Oh no," declared the woman as she huddled against the arm of the couch to protect herself. "No, no," she pleaded, as she hugged the couch, "I am afraid of dogs." But, oddly, she didn't get up to move away from him.

"Look at him," I urged softly. "He doesn't want to hurt you. He just wants to say hello." "No," she pleaded again. "I have never touched a dog." I tried to figure out how to resolve this, but was distracted by the ringing of the phone. When I turned back to the woman, to my astonishment she was quietly stroking Sammy's back! Sammy apparently had inched closer to her while my back was turned and was within touching distance. "Are you kidding?" was all I could muster.

"He's so sweet. I never touched a dog before," she said smiling. "He's so soft." She continued to pet him from his head to his back and he simply put his head down between his paws. He got what he wanted.

I looked at Sammy with awe. He was so determined to get this touch, this stroking, this recognition. He lay peacefully and allowed himself to be loved. He did this so many times over the years, with repairmen, my doormen and super, grocery delivery men. His only failure was a Time Warner cable repairman who insisted he wasn't scared of dogs, but would not lay a finger on Sammy, who was inching closer and closer, eventually lying down right in front of the man's feet. But, he never did get the cable guy to say hello. I could see his disappointment as his ears went down and so did his head.

This behavior was such an integral part of his nature. Never drawn to most dogs, Sammy was almost always drawn to the individuals at the other end of the leash.

CHAPTER 13

IS THAT THUNDER?

By late May Sammy and I had fallen into a chaotic, but sustainable routine. He had the run of the apartment and we had no more accidents. I was getting to know him, but as it turned out, I had a ways to go.

One late afternoon found us in the kitchen. The sun was still bright outside and it was a calm Saturday afternoon. I put dinner in Sammy's bowl and he was hungrily scarfing it down when it happened. A sound so enormous, it left me wondering if a gas main had exploded. It was a fearsome noise. Sammy, who was never distracted from food looked up at me with panic in his eyes.

His feet started to run, but on the tiled kitchen floor he couldn't get any traction and was frantically running in place. I pushed him from behind to give him some momentum when the second boom, louder than the first, caught us in the hallway. I dropped to my knees and wrapped my arms protectively around him and held on tight. He buried his head under my arm. He was shaking and panting. A third blast and I finally identified it as thunder, but there was no storm. It was as I learned later called dry thunder and it was, it seemed to Sammy, in our apartment.

He broke free of my hold and ran to the front door pawing and clawing at it. Wearing a camisole and no bra, I grabbed a rubberized jacket with a hood just in case and we fled into the elevator and out the front door of the building where life was going on as usual. No rain. Not a drop. No more thunder. It may have confirmed for Sammy what he already suspected. IT lived in our apartment. We went for a walk in very hot, humid air and me wrapped in rubberized clothing. In one of what turned out to a never ending series of firsts, I thought "to hell with it," peeled off the jacket from my D-cup chest and headed to the park. No one is looking at me, I reasoned, everyone was always looking at Sammy.

My best friend Anne told me after she saw Sammy for the first time that men would be flocking to me when they saw him and surely I would meet someone new. She was right. Men were flocking to me but they were totally into Sammy. "Is he a Dalmatian?" "How old?" "What was his name?" So, when I doffed my jacket, I was pretty secure in the knowledge that all eyes would be on him. In the meantime, I too, wondered what mix of breeds he was. Everyone we passed had an opinion even if they didn't express it to me. Little children would eye him in wonder, "Look Mommy, it's a fire dog," they said. "Can my son pet him?" mothers asked and I always said yes, provided the child didn't look aggressive. Sammy loved children and adjusted for them, sitting down or standing still to be adored.

The thunder turned into a real problem as we entered an especially loud spring and summer. At the first echo of thunder Sammy was already at the front door. No amount of food, treats, cajoling would distract him. He wanted out and out we went. More often than not the thunder was accompanied by pelting rain and lightning and we were confined to the lobby, where my dog's usual bravado evaporated into heavy panting, trembling and very hot doggy breath. This I know because I would sit beside him with my doorman on the cool tile floor and hold him. He could not be soothed and frequently didn't want to go back into the apartment. It was a struggle of enormous proportions.

I spoke to the vet. "Turn up the TV and the air conditioner," she said. That didn't help. She put him on medication called Clomicalm. It robbed him of his personality, but calm him, it did not. Constipate him it did. I found a form of plug-in product that was supposed to mimic Mommy dog pheromones. No help there. A dog therapist taught me a type of massage that was used to calm skittish horses. Complicated to execute, it didn't help. I took him off the Clomicalm.

My vet gave me Xanax, regular human grade Xanax. The trick, she explained was it took 45 minutes to work, so I had to try to time the storm. Let me say that NYC meteorologists were of no help in this regard. Doppler radar be damned, I either gave him the Xanax too early or too late. On July 4th we hit a double whammy, thunder and later on fireworks.

My Xanax-filled dog got on to extremely Jello-like legs, but fully alert and had to leave the apartment. Now! He wobbled to Broadway looking like a drunken sailor and people looked at us with a mixture of curiosity and puzzlement. What was wrong with this dog and why was this crazy woman making him walk??? Somehow we arrived home just in time for the first explosion of fireworks in the Hudson River. I was exhausted, but down to the lobby we went.

CHAPTER 14

NEVER SAY NO???

In late July with an overcast sky, but no rain in the forecast, Sammy and I headed out to the park. I watched the sky, because it looked ominous, but there was no rain, no distant rumbling. We headed deep into the park down a path that ran behind the Soldiers and Sailors monument. There were all sorts of smells here, little hills to climb, trees in need of watering, which Sammy supplied in abundance.

We found a new path, densely filled with grass and swirling dips and peaks to explore. On top of a particularly dense mound of dirt and grass, with no trees to shield us, Sammy squatted to poop and at that precise moment, the sky burst open with pelting rain, followed by a huge clap of thunder.

What happened next happened so fast my mind struggled to regain its balance. Mid poop, Sammy whirled around to face me and in the next instant pulled free of his collar and ran. He ran for his life it seemed and I ran after him screaming "Sammy." But, he didn't stop. He was galloping at a pace that was impossible to match. Already at least fifty yards ahead of me I saw his future crumble into a fatality either on Riverside Drive or the West Side Highway. At the rate he was running he could reach either before

I could reach him. This dog for whom I had struggled to find love, and who I now loved so intensely, was going to get hit by a car.

And, then something happened that I will never be able to explain. It felt as if a strong hand gripped my shoulder, holding me in place. I simply stopped running.

Instead, rooted to the spot, with rain streaming down my face, I screamed "No! Sammy, NO."And Sammy miraculously turned around, mid-run and looked back at me. "No," I shrieked again, "No." He paused again not sure of what to do, turned around and came back with panic in his beautiful brown eyes. I grabbed him with trembling hands by the scruff of his neck and held him until with the other hand I got the collar back on his neck. It was very loose from the rain and I knew I could lose him again. We ran up the steps leading to Riverside Drive. I held fast, I wasn't going to lose him now.

Across 89th street was an old mansion, now a school, with a giant, domed portico. We headed for that and found on one side a couple with an enormous, quaking golden retriever. We went to the opposite side where there were two steps. I sat down heaving, my breaths coming in long gasps and clutched Sammy, who was drenched to the core. He sat and I cradled him with both arms. How close I had been to losing him. It was unimaginable.

CHAPTER 15

SMILES

On one of our routine Sunday afternoon visits with my mother I found her lying on her side on her bed. She had a cold. Sammy bounded on the bed and found the crook of her knees and nestled in tight. "Sammy," my mother croaked, "you're going to crush me." But she moved slightly to accommodate his body and I could see both were happy. Oh, how she loved these moments with him.

At 92 everything, even a bad case of sniffles, was an event and my mother became weak easily. So I did for her what she had done for me when I was a child. I told her a story.

I told her about Sammy's very unusual markings. Her eyes were weak and she couldn't see what I was describing, so I explained that Sammy was literally covered in freckles and smudges and depending on the angle from which they were viewed they truly looked like dozens of dog faces; some looked like Sammy, but we also, through the years, spotted a variety of terriers, a few birds, and some spaniel-type faces, tongues lolling out or not and ears perked up or flopped down. It was as if Sammy was a receptacle for dozens of rescued animals! Finding faces on Sammy became a game everyone I knew played. "Ooh, look at this," someone would say, "look here's a butterfly," a dog walker once exclaimed.

Most outstanding of all were two singular features. Sammy had an enormous, clearly defined black heart on his back and moving down his right flank. It measured at least ten inches across. He was truly all heart. And, above his heart was the striking image of a very sinister looking woman, wearing what seemed to be a monocle, sporting shoulder length hair and a grim smile that stretched across her face. Sammy's heart formed what looked like a bustier to complete her bizarre look. As Sammy has aged, so has she.

"I have a dog who makes people smile," I continued my story. "Wherever we go, it seems he delights everyone. Smiles pop up on even the dourest faces." I told her about the one exception, a grizzled looking man of about 75, clad in a plaid shirt tucked half in and out of his baggy pants, who saw Sammy walking down the street. "What's that?" he yelled in my direction. I looked up at him as he was standing atop a set of stairs in front of a brownstone building.

"Excuse me," I said. "What's that?" he pointed at Sammy. "It's a dog," I said bristling. "That's the god damn ugliest dog I've ever seen," he proclaimed. "Yes," I said, "and thank you for that!" He was the exception. Everyone else tried to play the "what breed?" guessing game. Walking him turned into a social event, every time. If on a walk no one had stopped to admire or pet him, I could see his disappointment.

One day a gaggle of girls about 10 years in age approached us."Oooh," they crooned, as if in one voice, "what kind of a dog is that? Can we pet him?" Sammy, being a most accommodating creature and always happy to oblige little girls, promptly rolled onto his back for a belly rub. And, a belly rub he got. Small hands rubbed and tickled him everywhere and he was in ecstasy. An approaching tiny Yorkshire Terrier, seeing the commotion came and promptly smelled Sammy from the tip of his tail and upwards, a direction strictly forbidden by Sammy under normal circumstances. I believe he thought it was a little girl. In truth, Mugsy was the only dog who ever had this particular privilege!

The Yorkie, wanting in on a good thing, rolled over on his little back and got his share of adulation, unbeknownst to my dog. And, then everyone had to leave and there was Sammy, still on his back. I gently rubbed his soft belly and when he saw it was only me, he rose and looked around. I could almost hear him wonder, "Where did everyone go?"

I have always maintained that if a robber ever entered my apartment, Sammy would roll on his back and say "Just a quick rub and I'll tell you where the jewelry is!" My mother chortled with amusement at the thought.

I told her about Sammy and snow, because I knew this would bring more smiles to delight her. She listened in rapt attention, as I had as a child, to Beauty and the Beast or Cinderella. I said that surely if my dog could whoop and holler and slide down a snowy hill on his belly he would. Whoever said snow was made for children never had a dog. For most dogs, snow is heaven's bounty to be treasured until the last mound trickles slowly away into a dirty puddle. Pooping on top of a large mound of snow has to be the doggy equivalent of scaling Mt. Everest and planting a flag.

Sammy's eyes lit up when he exited our building and saw snow in the first year of our lives together. I, on the other hand was dumbstruck by the 22 inches that had accumulated overnight. The pavement and streets had disappeared and the cars were buried. Curiously, in the pristine white of the fresh snow, the only thing that was visible was the yellow pee streaks of the dogs who were out walking with their bundled up owners. None of them seemed as gleeful as their pets! I joined their ranks.

I had prepared for this adventure cobbling together the only attire I had in my closet that was remotely appropriate for snow. I looked as if I was wearing a haz mat suit! I had grabbed the infamous rubberized jacket with a hood and put a heavy winter coat on top of it. I knew it would be cold, but it was frigid and I hadn't put on a scarf. My fine Italian leather gloves offered zero protection and instantly my hands were numb. My boots; the only ones that had soles with grooves only came up past my ankles and snow was already working its way into them. I was frozen.

Some sweet soul had cleared a path the width of a snow shovel to my right, so off we went. Sammy was delirious with pleasure, pulling and tugging and coming up with a snout covered in snow. I had to laugh. And then we spotted a woman who looked to be over seventy, carrying two grocery bags, one in each hand. What on earth, I wondered, had possessed her to venture outdoors and in the same instant realized there was only room for one of us on this little path. I side stepped knee high into the snow to allow her to pass and Sammy dove into a snow bank, completely submerged except for the white tip of his tail. The next second he helicoptered out covered in fluffy snow with an expression of rapture on his face. Such happiness.

In that same year I became a devotee of dog catalogs; anything and everything relating to dogs was fodder for me and one day I came across a brown coat with fleece on the underside and a big, snap-on hood lined in fleece. I promptly ordered it and the next time it snowed Beatriz and I couldn't wait to put it on him and go out for a walk. As we exited the building, I flipped up the hood, to Sammy's surprise, and Beatriz and I giggled about this wonderful garment for it covered and protected him from his head to his tail. Sammy, on the other hand, though never averse to wearing coats, promptly shook off the hood, looked skyward and I could see joyfulness dance in his eyes. He wanted to feel the snow. As he grew older, he seemed to savor the protection the hood offered, but in the early years, he was like a child being told to wear mittens.

As soon as he could get free of this silly entrapment, he would. Eventually we bought this coat for Beatriz's dog as well.

My mother couldn't get enough. It was complete role reversal. I remembered how she would sit on the side of my bed and tell me stories as a child. "What goes around, surely does come around," I thought holding her hand.

I told her about Sammy's curiosity and the many forms it took. The street, of course, was a no brainer, but it was the unexpected places that Sammy couldn't wait to explore. Neighbors' apartments were of special interest, but he wasn't often granted access. One day, however, the apartment next door to mine became available. Empty of furniture, the door had been left open for a broker and we sneaked in. The apartment had at least seven or eight rooms and Sammy, off leash, zoomed past me and zipped from room to room before I could find him. Closets turned out to be his favorite find. He would dodge into a closet and sniff shelves and corners. Was this a mini apartment within an apartment he seemed to wonder? Once in the space, he couldn't wait to get in again, and so one day found us wandering from room to room when a broker with a potential buyer showed up unexpectedly. We were just rounding the corner of the dining room when we ran into a serious looking couple in their late 30's and their broker, a small man with a very bright tie.

I explained we were the next door neighbors, which certainly didn't bode well for this sale. Who would deliberately move into an apartment with this crazy duo already in residence? We exited as gracefully and apologetically as we could, at least I did. Sammy had other plans. He wanted to say hello, making matters worse, and I had to drag him away into the safety of our apartment. That couple did not buy the apartment. Surprise, surprise!

My mother laughed with delight. She wanted to see the dog catalogs. With her failing eyesight I had purchased a TV-like monitor with a built in magnifying apparatus and the next time we came over I brought a few catalogs with me. She loved the pictures of sleepy dogs lying in beds crafted especially for them. This very simple pleasure occupied her and made her feel even more a part of Sammy's life. How she cherished my dog!

CHAPTER 16

AN AMBASSADOR

I was beginning to appreciate Sammy and all of his many nuances and behaviors. I became finely tuned in, watching him, learning him. Aside from his unusual markings, I recognized that, unlike most dogs, Sammy wasn't just a "people person," but an ambassador of sorts. It almost seemed he knew that his purpose was to open people up, welcome them into his heart and extend his to them.

I began earnestly watching other dogs when we walked and while many of them exuded personality and were very happy to greet people, they didn't have the essential "Samminess," that my dog had. He approached every single person who stopped for him and I imagined if he had human language he would have started conversations. He would have asked how the person was, where were they going, what did they have planned? So engrossed was he in his passion for people, he often tried to walk with them after they were setting off in a direction we hadn't intended. He couldn't seem to get enough.

I observed the behavior of small breeds, who barked at Sammy a lot, and surmised that they didn't know what to make of the likes of a dog who didn't look like others. Larger dogs too, often looked puzzled when seeing Sammy. In their dog's view of the world, he must have seemed out of place and, for a few, his markings may have looked threatening. We all feel more comfortable with what we know. Sammy didn't conform to what dogs ought to look like I thought, trying to see him through a dog's eye. When people complimented me on his unique looks, I often said, "Tell him. He is not my creation." Saying thank you for something I didn't do, seemed odd. Whoever or whatever combined to create his extraordinary design had nothing to do with me. All I could do was admire him, along with everyone else. I had no ownership of his design any more than I did of him. I have always eschewed the word "owner," for I was not that. We were companions, two souls who lived together. There was no ownership except maybe Sammy's of me!

I also came to cherish the frequent, daily eye contact Sammy and I made over the years. I have since learned that a lot of dogs upon seeing someone they love, release in themselves, and in the person they are looking at, what is referred to as "the love hormone," or oxytocin. Scientists who study dogs say the release of this hormone induces feelings of happiness and, perhaps, that accounted for the warmth that I felt looking into his deep brown eyes. He was an old soul, I thought. A wise being in a fur suit.

CHAPTER 17

WHERE DO I GO???

My mother got over her cold, but in the years that ensued, any time she was in bed, Sammy nestled against her. He never did this with me. He seemed to sense that she needed this and my mother, who craved affection, loved it.

In the last five months of her life, my mother became unable to take care of her simplest needs. Her eyesight was deteriorating rapidly and her ability to move largely consisted of this makeshift arrangement of furniture she had devised to help her move around, literally clutching one armchair or table as she moved along. It was a recipe for disaster and sure enough, one night she tried to turn off her air conditioner in the dark and tripped over her walker. The assisted living facility decided the gash on her hand required an ambulance and they dispatched her before calling me. It was my first experience in an ER and everyone was busy trying to save a woman's life.

My mother demanded attention to her hand and the catheter, which they had inserted before I arrived. For what reason I do not know, but whoever had done the procedure didn't do it well. My mother, now in a curtained off area began trying to pull it out herself. When I tried but failed to quiet her, explaining a woman had stopped breathing, she began to yell "Nurse," at the top of her lungs. This wasn't the mother I was familiar with at all. She seemed more like a child and I didn't know how to behave with her.

Her wound was dressed and we returned home by "transport," a new word to add to my now growing vocabulary for my Mom. She needed 12, perhaps, 24 hour care to protect her from herself, though technically she wasn't ill, simply very old. While I had managed to take over all of her expenses for everything up until then, this added several thousand dollars per week was not in my purse.

Though I had always promised her I would never allow her to end up in a nursing home, I saw no alternative and I spoke to her doctor about how to accomplish this. He laid out a plan that included examining her and telling her he wanted to admit her to the hospital for some tests that could not be done in his office. She was not happy or cooperative. I had taken over and I realized slowly that she was reacting from a different part of her brain; the child brain without an adult's sensibility. It was difficult to explain anything to her yet dementia had not been ruled in. She was essentially herself, but somewhat vacant. But, she was stubborn and perhaps a bit belligerent. It made caring for her very difficult and it seemed to have happened so suddenly.

Life, however, always seem to have plans of its own and a day later as I was leaving work, the assisted living facility called to tell me my mother had choked while eating an omelet, turned blue and had stopped breathing, so they laid her on her side on the floor. I don't know why no one knew how to perform a Heimlich maneuver in an assisted living facility. So, not quite according to plan, my mother wound up in the hospital anyway.

She lay in the emergency room once again and when I got there I found my sweet mother in a curtained off area with her blonde wig pulled down over her eyes to protect her from the fluorescent lighting and wearing sunglasses. God help me, but she looked like Cousin It from the Addams Family. But, I understood that her eyes, due to macular degeneration, had become hyper sensitive to light. She was finally admitted her to a room where she lay untended to for three hours with me screaming in the hall to anyone wearing hospital scrubs. My best friend Anne, drove in from Long Island and tried to quiet me, but I was in a rage. How could they leave a 94 year old woman unattended? No one had even taken her pulse much less provided a blanket.

And so it began. She was admitted to the cardiac care unit and promptly taken off the medication she had been using for decades to thin her blood. I was fighting with everyone, because in truth I had lived her history and no one wanted to listen. Her incredibly swollen ankles I thought were the result of very tight thigh high stockings she had taken to wearing. Though a doctor wouldn't know to ask about thigh high anything, I knew how difficult it had been to remove them when I tried. They appeared to me to have forced her circulation into a very narrow corridor down her legs. I explained to the doctor that I thought she had inadvertently affected her circulation. He dismissed me until I insisted that he understand what she had done. He put compression stockings on her to her knees and in a day she had amazing-looking ankles. I wasn't sure what they were looking for, but what they found in the very last test, which should have been the first test on a choking victim, was that she had thrush, a fungus in her esophagus and, of course, nothing could go down. Had the doctor gone past that point he might have spied the ulcer that wound up ending her life.

In the meantime, because Sammy was getting over yet another bout of giardia, I kept plying him with Flagyl to keep his bowel movements in check. He missed our Sunday walk to the Esplanade to visit with my mother and looked confused. How he knew what day of week it was I have never understood.

My mother was released to an interim facility, called a rehab, while I could find a nursing home. Surprisingly, Sammy was allowed to visit. She was thrilled to see him, but he faltered a bit when he tried to jump on her bed. I parked it away in my head, but when he had trouble jumping into my car, I became alarmed. I watched him and over the next few days his gait became uneven, his back was arching and he had trouble walking. I took him to the vet where they thought it was an orthopedic issue, but just told me to keep an eye on him. A day later when my doorman had to carry him into the lobby I went into a fall blown panic.

I called the vet and they sent over a strong male nurse who carried Sammy to a taxi and then to the clinic, with me trailing behind helplessly. This was the first time something like this happened and in the nurse's arms, Sammy looked at me with an unreadable expression. It looked helpless and accepting all at the same time. His leash dragged behind, trailing to the street and I rushed to pick it up to let him know I was still attached. No one knew what was wrong. And, I had to rush to the rehab to look after my mother, because in this hideous facility on 106th street, they neglected her, did everything but help her and I was scared they would wind up killing her because they switched all her medication again. They were like a storage depot for old, frail bodies. While she was in their care for three weeks, my mother lost 23 pounds.

For five days I ran from the rehab to the vet. No one was getting better. Our favorite vet called in a neurologist and I was afraid of what the diagnosis would be. Multiple Sclerosis? Did dogs even get that? I raced up to the rehab and fought with a nurse because my mother looked pale and unwell and I got nowhere. It was as if they had admitted her to a psych ward, but the medical staff were the crazy people.

I ran back to the vet. It was eight in the evening and when I arrived my vet walked towards me. I couldn't read her expression. "We have a diagnosis," she said. I blanched. "No, it's good," she reassured me. As it turned out, in my zeal to keep Sammy from developing diarrhea I had caused something called Flagyl Toxicity.

His liver couldn't process all the medication and fixing him simply required taking him off the drug. If only more things in life were that simple. In three days with a boost of Valium to stabilize his gait and balance, I had my guy back. His back slowly lost the arch and he was okay. My mother was not.

I was fortunate to have a cousin who was married to a wealthy man who had donated large amounts of money to a beautiful nursing home in Westchester. He used his considerable influence to get them to take my mother, but the process was slow. I ran through the machinations of Medicaid and prayed that I would never wind up like this. My mother was accepted and was given a beautiful private room with its own bathroom. I was so relieved, but she didn't seem to register her surroundings. Her age had begun to show in powerful ways. She lost her lovely, ladylike graciousness and I realized I was having a terrible problem accepting her as a very old person. Not for the first did I become aware that I wasn't very capable in the area of old age. I didn't know this would come back to haunt me in the years ahead.

She and I were both delighted though to discover that here, as was the case in the rehab, Sammy was welcome to visit. He had to pass a "Therapy Dog" test and wear a little bandana to identify him on the premises. He always jumped into her bed whenever we visited. This became our new Sunday destination.

Whenever we went to the nursing home, traveling its narrow, bumpy two lane road Sammy seemed to sense that my mother was near. He couldn't wait for us to get cleared at the gate and once parked, he bounded out of the car, ready for adventure. The building that my mother was in was huge, with beautiful art gracing the walls, and even a large set of wooden train cars always in motion on rickety tracks behind a faux picket fence, as in a department store window. Sammy's eyes danced as he watched the trains chug along, and to my horror, once tried to raise his leg on the fence. I could understand his reasoning. All the fences he knew were located outside and were fair game, so why not here? I prayed no one saw us.

In the nursing home people's faces lit up when they saw him. He drew a crowd, but so engrossed was he in all the new smells and room after room to explore, that my "Therapy Dog," barely stopped long enough to perform any "therapy." One day he dragged me into what I presumed was an empty room, only to find a very frail, old man asleep on his back in his bed. He opened his eyes just as Sammy approached him, yelled out a strangled series of vowels and we ran and hid in my mother's room. I only hoped the man might have thought he had had a nightmare.

My solace during this turbulent time turned out to be the acres of lush green grass that surrounded the various buildings that made up the nursing home. The lawns bordered on the Hudson River, and Sammy I roamed the property eventually sitting down in the grass every weekend. The river soothed my frantic soul and appeared to have charmed Sammy as well with its quiet.

Here I could think, or not, and calm my fears which were mounting daily. I had been brought up in a home that didn't express anger and so I was very surprised that in this phase of my life I found that I had anger in abundance and a voice that delivered it in decibels. My mother needed an advocate and I plunged into this role as I always have for my dog; pushing back when things didn't make sense and when no one really seemed to care.

CHAPTER 18

ALL THINGS MUST END

My mother, at 94, who hadn't been sick with the exception of old age issues, developed a bleeding ulcer. Rushed to a nearby hospital and given four transfusions, she wound up in the ICU and died at 5 o'clock the following morning. It was so sudden. She was gone and for at least a year, every Sunday, Sammy tried to walk me over to the assisted living facility to visit her. It was heartbreaking. I came to understand that my dog's routines with humans were sacred to him. He depended on them as he depended on seeing Beatriz every weekday. He seemed to anticipate every coming and going and without my mother to visit he was perplexed and sad.

My mother was buried near a tree, because she loved trees, and after a year, as is the rite in Jewish tradition, a flat slab of bronze was laid down to mark her grave. Ordered a year before, I had forgotten what it was to look like. The suddenness of her death and all the activity that fell on me, as the only child, made everything murky.

The funeral home notified me that the stone was now in place and ready to be unveiled. I didn't invite anyone, but I went to talk to my Mom. I didn't go alone, however. My housekeeper, Beatriz, her husband, Alberto, a limo driver, and Sammy, piled into Alberto's car and drove to Westchester. Though not a custom in this cemetery we stopped so I could buy flowers. I bought bright red peonies and other colorful flowers which I knew she would have loved. Dogs were not allowed in the cemetery, though it wasn't spelled out anywhere, but I thought maybe Sammy would somehow sense her. What I didn't expect was that I couldn't find her.

I looked for the tree, but it had been a year, and Beatriz and I fanned out while Alberto strode around with Sammy. Frantic I called the cemetery and told them where I was. They re-directed me and finally I found the bronze marker. I had chosen well I realized. A rush of falling bronze stars formed the outer perimeter of the stone and I had used the Hungarian spelling of her name to write *"Klari Lane, Cherished Mother and Wife."* I noticed a small hole not much larger than a pencil eraser at the top of the stone and was about to lay down the flowers when Beatriz said "No, wait." I watched in horror as she stuck her finger in the hole and began to twist her finger around. "What are you doing?" I whispered, not knowing what this hole would release, when she pulled out an earth-encrusted object that turned out to be an urn.

I had ordered an urn? I had no idea. With this in hand she walked to the side of the path and turned on a spigot. Ah, I thought. In my many visits to this cemetery, as my grandmothers were buried here as well, I had never understood the spigots. Now, I watched her clean off the soil and pour water in. She brought it back to me, took the flowers, put them in and twisted the urn into the stone, right side up now. Sammy came over and sniffed. I wondered again if he knew some part of her was here. But, then he ran with Alberto to smell a tree. Beatriz gave me time to commune with my mother and when I brushed away my tears, she went to the grave, genuflected and said a prayer. She had loved my mother.

I watched, as if once removed, and started to smile. How my mother, who wasn't averse to breaking rules once in a while, would have loved this scene. Here we were in a fairly religious section of this vast cemetery and only her grave had a wild rush of dazzling bright flowers issuing from it. And, here she was with a crazy black and white dog peeing on trees to his heart's content, while a Colombian woman crossed herself at her grave. My mother would have taken such pleasure in this totally irreverent tableau.

CHAPTER 19

BEATRIZ

My housekeeper, Beatriz deserves a book, not just a chapter. She has been Sammy's second Mom from Day 1. Hailing from a small town in Colombia, South America, she speaks in choppy Beatriz English. I wouldn't care if she spoke Swahili. She adores Sammy. He, to this day, cannot control his sheer pleasure at the sight of her and he gets to see her five days a week. He barks this pleasure at her every morning. No one else, including me, gets this greeting. With an extraordinary, genuine smile, wavy dark hair down to her waist, Beatriz is beautiful inside and out.

Not simply a housekeeper, she is the keeper of our lives, Sammy's and mine. Between her "Ai carico," "Ai, carrumbas," "tramposo," and "su assay a la cama," she has transformed my dog into a bilingual quadruped. She has been through the best and worst of our time together and has become family in the very deepest sense of the word.

We didn't start our relationship on a five day a week basis. Rather, Beatriz began working for me because my long time housekeeper was retiring. So, Beatriz would come one day a week and was already ensconced before Sammy arrived.

She often reminds of the day I asked her if she liked dogs, because guess who was in my guest room!! Unbeknownst to me, in the days when Sammy spent the daylight hours in that room, Beatriz would go in and play with him or smuggle him out for a walk. She also could not understand my failure to bond back then. She apparently loved him at first sight!

Through all of my ups and downs and scares with my dog, Beatriz has been there, laughing and crying with me and loving my dog with a heart as big as a universe. She is the essence of kindness and I have been so blessed to have her in my life.

CHAPTER 20

A SHOPPING DOG

Without our Sunday visits with my mother Sammy and I went on extensive walks on Broadway. Usually off limits because of the sheer amount of food people carelessly threw on the street, I was feeling more confident and Sammy, it appeared, loved to shop! I had a shopping dog.

So, we looked for signs of welcome which usually came with the absence of huge letters saying "No dogs allowed." We went into stores exploring and sometimes actually buying things I actually didn't really need. We discovered that Talbot's, a clothing chain, welcomed dogs and even had a big bowl of communal water to offer. I never allowed him to partake as my very prone-to-infection dog could have picked up anything from the water, but Sammy was more interested in the clothes. He would sniff through display after display of colorful pants, skirts, any low lying garments. But, his biggest delight was in the two overstuffed red arm chairs that were located near the front of the store. Yes, I allowed my dog to jump in the chairs and settle in for a snooze. As long as I kept looking as if I was going to make a purchase, we got away with it. It was a great place to visit because the AC was strong and it was very hot outside.

Then, at last a security guard got wise and we were unceremoniously booted out of Talbot's. Not very worried, we moved on to a store that carried towels, linens, trash cans, soap, and furniture. It didn't take too long before he was knocking over any low hanging fruit. To their credit, they never threw us out, but I was always apologizing and re-stocking shelves.

The pet store was an entirely different matter. All bets were off. As at the vet's office, everyone at the pet store recognized Sammy's bark. He, being the wise animal he was, knew a treat when he smelled one, not to mention bully sticks, pig's ears and other assorted, completely off limit items that had him drooling from the moment we set our six feet in the store. A chorus of "Hi Sammy," greeted us every time and they kindly gave us the treats he was allowed to eat. Utterly out of control in this environment, Sammy managed to scare off customers, small dogs and even the resident cat, who one would think had seen all sorts of black and white beasts before.

But, really nothing compared to our first trip to PetCo, where Sammy explored every sort of rodent by standing on his hind legs and staring into their glass enclosures. If he was bad in our local pet store, he was a maniac at PetCo, where all sorts of treats in every possible color, shape and size were located at eye level – doggy eye level that is, in bins near the floor. People actually got out of our way as I apologized my way to the cash register with his favorite toys in hand. Cute, yes, but for someone who liked to maintain control over situations, it was not amusing. I would exit the store panting, chanting "Never again," a familiar mantra, until the next time, when invariably I convinced myself that the time before wasn't as bad as I remembered. And, inevitably I took Sammy with me the next time I went to Petco, because truthfully, when I went by myself, it didn't feel the same.

But, wow, I was walking a lot. Not that that's a bad thing, but I was also running a business and I needed help, more than I had or that Ellen could provide.

CHAPTER 21

A WORD . . .OR TWO,
ABOUT DOG WALKERS

If Sammy was a handful for me, he proved to be a challenge for some dog walkers as well. And, many of them proved to be a challenge for me. I live in New York City where there must be ten walkers per square foot of pavement, but experience taught me, and many times the hard way, that if you're going to trust someone with your dog, they need to earn your trust.

I knew nothing in the beginning. Now I'm a pro. I learned that virtually anyone who wants to earn money walking your dog will invariably drop to their knees to sing the praises of your pup. I finally stopped being fooled by this. They want your money, I told myself. Don't just hand over your dog. So, I paid for their time and took the first one or two walks with them. I showed them what it is like to walk, as in my case, with a high spirited nut job who wants to eat and smell everything on the street and pee on it too.

Not all dogs are created equal and in the walking department my dog excelled. So in the beginning when I decided I wanted some downtime now and then I hired dog walkers for various times of the day. What I learned? Few people want to walk dogs when the sun goes down. But, the bad walkers abounded day and night and with

Sammy I learned to trust my instincts and my neighbors, and other people who walked their dogs around the time Sammy walked. They are great observers.

In the first year I ran through walkers like water. It went something like this:

Jerry

Nice guy, late 50's, prematurely stooped shoulders and big, bushy brown hair, Jerry came referred by a card he deposited with my vet's reception desk. Ironically, was he "vetted" by my vet? No! Jerry showed up, presumably to qualify for walking Sammy twice a week at 11 PM. In our interview he told me I was feeding Sammy very bad food and extoled the virtues of a brand I wasn't familiar with. The lecture went on for 45 minutes. Did we discuss Sammy? Not so much. Did Jerry ever arrive at the designated time. Hmmm, can't exactly remember that happening. But, Sammy seemed to like him, so out we went for our trial run.

Jerry seemed to get Sammy's manic street behavior and was calm about walking him. Our one to two nights a week rapidly morphed into six. During the time I knew him, Jerry's dog of 15 years died and he would not let go of the idea that the vet hadn't done the right things. Was that true? I couldn't know, but the saga rolled on and on and "did I know a lawyer?" and "could I write a letter," and on and on. Then one day I ran into one of the women to whom I had tried to give Sammy in the park very early on. We had become street pals. She told me that she had watched Jerry walking Sammy in the park on several occasions always muttering angrily to himself and not seeming quite right. I parked this information but didn't act on it immediately.

Then came the evening that Jerry came in my front door and had no patience for Sammy's "rub my belly before we walk," routine. He flipped Sammy upright. But, Sammy being the righteous being he is, promptly went back to belly up position. Jerry flipped him again amidst my protestation of "hey, he's not a hamburger," and the next thing I knew Sammy had Jerry's hand between his teeth. Dear God, I thought, he is a Pit Bull after all. Calmly though, Jerry assured me Sammy wasn't biting him, he was simply holding his hand to stop the flipping. Wow, I was impressed by my dog.

Then after I too could see a mounting aura of "angry" around Jerry, he came to pick up Sammy, who was in my bedroom on my bed, and Sammy didn't want to go. I persuaded him nonetheless and out they went. The next night Sammy absolutely refused to leave my bed and I finally listened to him. I walked back to my foyer and told Jerry that Sammy didn't want to walk with him anymore. Jerry seemed not to understand. I paid him and told him we were finished and pretty much escorted him out my front door. I waited about ten minutes and finally said to Sammy, "Want to go for a walk?" He bounded off the bed and we headed to the lobby only to find Jerry there talking to my doorman. He stretched out his hand as if to take the leash.

"No," I said. "Sammy does not want to walk with you tonight or any other night." We emerged into a torrid, humid September night where rats and giant roaches abounded and I kept looking over my shoulder. The next morning I received two screaming calls from Jerry. And, suffice it to say, was left walking my dog and afraid to turn into any side street for fear Jerry was stalking me.

I hired my relief doorman, Edwin, to "tail" me, which was difficult considering he is six foot six inches and a generally big guy. But, he was a super-spy. I would turn around to see him and he was invisible. He did this with me for two nights until I felt safe enough to go out alone.

. . . *Kathy, The Burnt-Out Case and Unintelligible Greek Woman*
I have lumped these people together because they formed a daisy chain of craziness. First, came Kathy, wearing a cowboy hat and jangling at least 50 keys from her jeans. I liked her and she liked

Sammy, but didn't want to walk him, it was too late, he was too strong, he ate poop (who could keep their eyes so trained on him to stop this and was it really her job?) and she knew someone else to recommend.

So I opened my front door to the Burnt-Out Case, a skinny woman in her 20's with incredibly dark circles around her eyes, who slumped on my foyer floor, hugged Sammy, asked which shelter he came from and burst into tears. "Oh My God, did I know how terrible these poor dogs were treated there?" and "Oh My God, they kept these skinny pit bulls in the back and they weren't fed well and they were put to sleep before anyone could adopt them." I offered Kleenex. Sammy was all over her. My, I thought, he likes her. Turned out he liked the "Chicken Strips" dog treats she had in every pocket. Sitting on my floor, dressed all in black, she looked like an exhausted rag doll, but I hate to admit, I let Sammy walk with her.

She showed up again the following night and looked seriously strung out, to the point that I asked, as she once again slumped on my floor, "Are you taking anything?" Startled, she asked me why I was asking. I explained that her collapsed, weepy posture concerned me. "No," she assured me weakly, she just found out a friend she knew had died. Of an overdose, I wondered? This time I refused to let her walk Sammy.

End of Burnt-Out Case. Enter Unintelligible Greek Woman.
Kathy sent me someone new, a plumpish, middle-aged, distinctly foreign woman bundled in an impossibly over-sized down jacket, who couldn't speak English. Try explaining no poop eating to someone who doesn't speak the same language. Okay, I said, pointing to the door. I will walk with you. That she seemed to understand, but it didn't appear to please her, nor did my numerous attempts to wrest Sammy's leash away from her in the bitter cold as he lunged for what came to be known to me as "poopsicles," tiny "morsels" of

poop, frozen and buried in the snow. Crafty, crafty dog!!!!! Greek lady resigned on the spot and left us on the street corner.

There were so many strangers that passed through our lives until we arrived at our current crew, who, God bless them, have been with us for three years or more and have patience for my now 13 ½ year old Sammy. But, it took a long, long time to find these treasured few. But, before them, there were . .

Berty, Eric, and at the top of my "I wish I could strangle" list, Marco.
Berty entered our life as a former, but still hopeful, mid-40's actress, who had recently lost her beloved dog to cancer. She immediately tried to turn Sammy into her deceased dog, Moonshine. Sammy was not, nor has ever been the step-in for any other dog. But, my dog was very compliant as long as things pretty much resembled his routine. I had strict rule about no treats on the street, never wanting to give him the idea that eating anything on the street was okay. But, Berty thought otherwise. While Sammy's favorite street treat was poop, Berty decided she could distract him with doggy kibble. Not so much. Berty and I had our first fight.

Next she appeared one day with what I could only interpret as the kind of harness used for Seeing Eye dogs. Our second fight! Finally, a unique thought occurred to me around walk number seven or maybe eight. He's my dog, I realized, and I, and only I, will decide what he eats, where he eats it and what kind of paraphernalia he will wear. Our third fight and it was loud. It ended with Berty pointing her index finger to the sky and screaming at me, "No dog will eat anything off the street on my watch." And, out the door they went, Sammy still wearing his usual collar.

I made a bet with myself. "For sure," I thought, Berty will come back with some kind of horror story, and she did not disappoint. They arrived earlier than usual and the moment they entered the apartment it began . . ."We were only feet from the building when

Sammy picked up a chicken bone and I had to force it out of his mouth," she proclaimed, triumphant!

Now, not for nothing and certainly a chicken bone could have been tossed on the street around my house, however, I live in a pretty nice part of Manhattan with a doorman tasked with keeping our half of the block clean. They were always hosing and sweeping the street. Could the doorman on duty have missed a random chicken bone? Certainly. Was it likely to have happened on exactly this particular walk? I thought not. "This isn't working for me," I calmly explained to Berty, who was now in full lather. "Sammy is going to die," she ranted, "and it will be your fault." "Goodbye," I said. And, escorted her out the door.

I needed to find a mid-morning walker, because Sammy still seemed to need to walk six to seven times a day. So, now walkerless, the next day I walked my precious craziness before going to work. We lived on 83rd street and when we reached the corner of 86th street I saw a pleasant looking man, about average height, a baseball cap, cargo shorts with a caramel and white spotted spaniel. Upon seeing Sammy he dropped to his knees (I should have recognized the gesture by then, but no), and proclaimed Sammy to be the most extraordinary dog he had ever seen. I told him his dog was beautiful too, and he quickly reassured me, it wasn't his, but he was walking it.

"Ah, you're a dog walker," I assessed quickly, "tell me about yourself." He told me with somewhat thickly accented English, that his name was Marco and he was from Romania. "Did he have room for another dog?" I asked, adding I could keep him very busy if he had time. He did, because as it turned out he was pretty new to this occupation.

And so a three year relationship began. He had to travel from another borough, but was also pretty much on time and wound up walking Sammy three times a day, seven days a week. I became his surrogate mother! Oy, his back hurt. Oy, his eye hurt. Eeeiii, he had a stabbing pain down the leg. He needed aspirin. He needed help choosing sunglasses for his mother, who was milking him long distance for everything from a new refrigerator to a TV. He, an illegal immigrant, hadn't seen her in 17 years. We celebrated his Orthodox versions of Christmas and Easter. He became a part of our daily lives.

Then, the seven days became, understandably too much. We went down to six. One morning, in what should have set off all sorts of warning bells in me, he showed up with a duffle bag tossed over his shoulder. "Look," he said, unzipping the top, "look what I have." The head of a tiny Yorkshire terrier poked out of the opening, panting and struggling to get out. "Marco," I exclaimed, "how long has this dog been in there?" 'Oh, only a few hours," he said, "I have to take him to his owner. The dog stayed in my apartment last night."

I lifted the tiny dog out of the bag and it began scurrying up my hallway, peeing every couple of seconds. Sammy watched this spectacle with what I can only call unabashed doggy amusement. "Just wait," I could almost hear him thinking. "She ain't gonna' put up with that." And I didn't. I brought the dog some water and turned to face Marco. "What were you thinking?" I asked. "You have to take this dog home." It was August of our second year together and in the high 90's outdoors.

The next day came a call from a neighborhood dog walker, who knew Sammy. Everyone, it seemed, knew Sammy. Her English was tinged with a southern inflection. She was furious. "You know that walker you have, Marco something? He tied up your dog to a parking meter outside Zabar's, while he sat inside their café sipping coffee and don't let him tell you otherwise," she yelled. "He coulda' got your dog strangled, the leash was so tight to the meter," she went on. "Someone could have stolen him. I would fire his ass," she concluded. Marco brought Sammy home.

He had violated two of my cardinal rules. No tying up my dog for any reason and no walking on Broadway. I waited for his version of the story and out it came. "I know you going to get call from this fat, black walker," he began, "but she's crazy. I couldn't take Sammy into Zabar's and he needed water," he explained. "It was for a minute, but when I came out she was screaming at me." I believed her, not him. "Listen," I said, "here's the deal. If you ever take Sammy out for a walk and come back without him, I will kill you. I may be 20 years older than you and a woman, but I promise I will kill you." In my neck of the US dogs were often snatched and used to train Pit Bulls to become attack dogs. With his gentle nature and extraordinary markings, he would be an easy target. I was rattled, but how would I replace Marco? I gave him one more chance, believing in my heart he wouldn't be stupid enough to do this again. I was wrong.

A young woman, who worked for my agency moved into a building around the corner from Zabar's that winter. One day and rather timidly she began, "Does Sammy have a brown winter coat?" she asked. "Yes, I said, "why?" "Well, I feel bad saying this, because maybe I am wrong and I don't want to cause trouble, but I think I saw Sammy tied up outside of Zabar's on my way home last night after work," she said. "I couldn't tell for sure because the coat covered so much of him, but I almost untied him to take him home. It was so icy and windy last night." I thought my head would pop open!

My office was the last in a row of offices at my agency and I stormed to my desk and called Marco. "Did you tie up Sammy to a meter outside of Zabar's again?" I demanded. "When?" he asked in return.

My rage could be heard down the row of offices. "Wrong answer," I roared at him. "What do you mean when? How many times have there been?" He tried, but I didn't let him get a word in. My heart was flooded with relief that I still had Sammy, home and safe, but the awful reality of what could have happened to him flushed over me like a fever. "You have to be the most stupid person alive,"

I continued my rant. "The money you earn from me pays your rent. How could you pretend to love my dog and do this? You're fired," I screamed. "If you ever see me on the street," I said in parting "stay very far away." In the weeks that followed I learned that he had also tied up my dog outside of Circuit City, Filene's Basement and who knows where else? Street vendors were happy to fill in the details as I passed them in the weeks after.

And then there was Eric, for two weeks . . .
As it is with dog walkers, people know people who know a dog walker and thus I discovered Eric, a personable, young Israeli guy, who loved dogs, he said, and would be happy to come from Brooklyn every night and walk my dog. He worked as a computer programmer during the day and wanted extra cash. Sammy seemed to like Eric. I performed my perfunctory initial walk and saw that Eric knew how to handle a leash.

Two weeks in, I got a call from an upstairs neighbor, who had a female dog named Lucy. Lucy and Sammy didn't seem to like each other and performed some sort of growling ritual when seeing one another. Oddly, it was the only time I ever heard Sammy growl.

"I hate to make this call," Lucy's owner prefaced, "But I would want to know if anyone was hurting my dog." Alarmed, I asked her to continue. "Well, you know how Sammy and Lucy growl at each other, right? So, Sammy was approaching the building and I was standing there with Lucy and they growled and your walker punched Sammy in the head."

I went blind with fury. Sammy was safely home, but Eric was due to come again the next night. I picked up the phone and called him, barely able to speak with anger frothing at my lips.

"You punched my dog in the head," I stated. "Well, what was I supposed to do?" he asked, "He was growling at another dog." "No one hurts my dog," I raged at him. "Pick up the money I owe you at the front desk and never let me see you again," I slammed down the phone. Was there anyone I could trust?

I was very surprised at how easy to anger I was over Sammy. I didn't really recognize the place from which this kind of rage emanated inside of me. In protection of Sammy, all bets were off. I was fierce and formidable. I wouldn't want to have crossed me and I was very mystified by where this side of me had resided all my life. Perhaps, it took the love of this special creature to tap into this well. It has never stopped.

CHAPTER 22

AT LAST, SANITY!!

I began to scout for a new nighttime walker, but this time by watching dog walkers on the street. Looking for sane dog walkers had become a part time occupation for me. I watched their attentiveness, how much leash they gave their dogs, how patient they were, or weren't. Some walkers, walking three dogs or more, would keep up their stride without regard to their charges, who literally had to pee and walk at the same time. Not for me, I thought.

But, one day right in front of my building, I spotted a thirty-ish looking woman with a beautiful golden braid of hair trilling softly down her back. She was walking a single dog and seemed to really care about the dog's needs and I followed her for two blocks to make sure it wasn't a fluke. But, she seemed like the real deal. I approached tentatively, because in my quest to find the perfect walkers I have sometimes confused an owner with a walker to some level of indignation on the owner's part.

"Excuse me," I said walking up to her. "Are you a walker?" Yes, she was, she said, did I need one? "Oh God, yes," I responded and she laughed. "Yeah, there are some really bad apples out there, you have to be careful. What kind of dog do you have?" Hmmmm, I thought, would I extol the glorious virtues of Sammy or cut to the chase with the poop eating. I opted for the former. So, Jocelyn entered our lives, but only for a second. She lived over twenty blocks away and walked dogs all day. As much as she admired and liked Sammy, it was too much for her, but she knew someone else, who she recommended highly. Michele. Dear Lord, I thought, here we go yet again.

As had become our habit, Sammy obligingly met every new walker by the elevator on our landing. He quite literally sat, facing the elevator door, excited to see anyone who emerged and ecstatic when it was for him. And so we met Michele. Raven haired and 1940's movie star beautiful, she was petite and had a lovely smile. She did the requisite bending of the knees, but spoke directly to Sammy, cradling his face in her hands. "He is beautiful," she exclaimed at last looking up at me, "what mix is he?" I shrugged as I really didn't know.

Michele, it turned out was new to the dog walking business. Highly educated, she had been part of a downsizing at a major brokerage firm and had been the lucky beneficiary of a retiring walker's clientele. She also had a dog, named Oliver and they both entered our lives, she as Sammy's nighttime walker and Ollie as Sammy's walking partner.

Black from snout to tail, Ollie, A Chow and Lab mix, formed a striking contract to Sammy's black and white coat. Almost the same height, they walked down the street, bumping side to side. Skittish outdoors, Ollie's destination was always the park as that's where he felt safe enough to do his business. Sammy was delighted for an extra walk in the park. Michele, it turned out, was sane, funny and a keeper, I prayed. We felt whole. She became part of our little family although these days no longer walking dogs, with the exception of Sammy.

Michele, Ollie, Ellen and Mugsy helped us usher in Sammy's ninth birthday and like little children at a party, they were insanely excited and ready to celebrate. I had toys for all of them, food and plenty of space for their antics and when all was over my apartment looked like a storm of white toy stuffing had rained from the sky. The toys, if you could call them that at the end, were eviscerated from seam to seam. The living room and foyer were blanketed in clouds of white fluff and the three dogs were exhausted and simply lying on the floor, all snouts turned to an invisible center.

For me, the most memorable part of that night was when everyone was arriving. Ollie and Michele arrived first. We told them that Mugsy was coming and opened the door. Sammy and Ollie sat side by side in the doorway, because they understood they were being joined by another, expectant and excited and when the elevator door opened and Mugsy flew out, blowing by the two of them, they took off after her, running from room to room, throwing off waves of happiness and exaltation.

Michele has been a witness to a lot of Sammy's life and in his old age, Ollie has overtaken him in size and height. As with human friends, Sammy and Ollie have had their differences, though usually over Sammy's toys, and for a short while after Ollie took a toy out of Sammy's mouth, it looked to me as if Sammy had a Tony Soprano "blue moon in his eyes," whenever he saw Ollie. So, for a while the friendship was interrupted, as I didn't know how to interpret Sammy's expression when he looked at Ollie; actually glowered at him.

At first, Ollie chose to ignore Sammy's hard stare, opting instead to gleefully fly through the air landing on my sofa and rolling around in positions that looked so wild and delirious I thought he would hurt his neck. He jumped in Sammy's bed, ate his treats when proffered and was having a high old time, but I told Michele I was concerned, because I had never seen Sammy look at another dog this way and I was worried that a war might erupt. It almost had twice before but was averted with Michele's and my intervention. Eventually, though the years and age mellowed them both and peace was restored.

Michele, who had become invested in determining Sammy's breed(s), presented me with a birthday present one year. A DNA test for Sammy, cheek swab and all, it would finally answer the question "what is he a mix of?" She swabbed, I put all the requisite information and swabs in the envelope the company provided and we waited and waited for the result. Finally, it arrived and I was stunned to discover that my then 67.8 pound dog was a mix of a dachshund, Pomeranian and Chihuahua. Michele and I laughed until we cried. I contacted the lab by email and included a photo of Sammy, explaining that this had to have been a mistake. They obligingly sent me a free kit to run the test again.

The second time was no better than the first. This time it included a Parson's Russell Terrier. It turned out the DNA banks were only as good as the DNA samples they had on file and Pit Bulls (Staffordshire Terriers) and an Australian breed, called Catahoula, were not in their system, hence Sammy's Levels 1 and 2, which would have been the most prominent, were unavailable for testing. I stumbled across a picture of an Australian Catahoula quite by accident trolling the Internet one day and there was my sweet Sammy. Except for that image, I have never encountered another dog who even comes close to resembling my guy. I have, though, since discovered that there are Louisiana and Alabama Catahoula and while I see a resemblance, they are not black and white like Sammy and I have to believe the Pit Bull ancestry may account for the color differences. Chihuahua, indeed!!!!! It seems his ancestors may have been a very busy lot!

CHAPTER 23

THE MOVE

And then our lives took a turn.

As it was for many people in 2008 and 2009, when the bottom fell out of the economy, my PR business, which spanned three decades, began to wobble. I stressed about money all the time. I let staff members go. My life seemed to implode. And so, I decided to sell my apartment, a home I had known from childhood. Although I had moved out in my twenties, I had moved back in when my parents retired to Florida. My apartment was witness to my marriage and subsequent divorce. My grandmother's bedroom became home to my step-daughter. My parent's bedroom became mine. It was Sammy's home and now it was on the market.

I was barely able to make ends meet until the apartment sold for far less than the price at which it had been listed. My best friends loaned me money to cover the stretch from contract to closing, a span of five months. I needed to find a new place to live and took Sammy wherever I went. I wanted to stay in my neighborhood, but was only interested in renting.

I finally settled on a one bedroom three blocks from where I lived in a building undergoing renovation on the corner of 82nd street and Riverside Drive. I was promised the moon in a 61 page lease, but moved into hell instead. The one page, yes, in fine print, that talked about the rights the landlord had during the period of renovation somehow were hidden under the promises of a rooftop terrace and basement gym. The reality was the water for the entire building was turned off almost every other day and the two elevators that were supposed to service my side of the building had been reduced to one. But, I didn't know any of this.

I took Sammy to our new home every day to get him acclimated and he, being the nosy guy that he is, seemed to love it; New closets to explore, new people to adore him; A quarter of a block away from the park.

Life seemed good and then it went very bad.

Two nights before we were scheduled to move, Sammy began vomiting. My dog didn't vomit unless he was really sick. I called the vet. It was 11 PM. The on call vet called me back. "Wait until morning," she advised. "No," I insisted, "he is really sick." She grudgingly, met us at the clinic and admitted him. I could hear him barking for me as I left. I was scared to death. According to the vet, he continued to vomit throughout the night accompanied by explosive diarrhea. My favorite vet was no longer with the practice and my new doctor strongly urged an ultrasound as x-rays were failing to show the cause of the sickness. Perhaps he swallowed something?

Bloodwork, a fecal test and an ultrasound revealed a lot. My crazy dog once again had giardia, but this time it had saved his life, because the ultrasound showed a greatly enlarged spleen with a mass inside. My vet was on the fence about the prognosis. We wouldn't know until they removed his spleen and the mass, and time was of the essence. If the engorged spleen didn't come out it might burst and Sammy would bleed to death. Surgery was scheduled for the day I had to move. I was dizzy and strangled with fear. I couldn't breathe.

As movers roiled around me in my old apartment, I felt helpless. The sounds of packing tape being stretched and slapped on boxes echoed around me, but Sammy fully occupied my entire head. Did he have cancer? Was the mass cancer? I walked over to the vet to visit with my guy and talked to the vet. If it was cancer I told her please do not let him wake up. My eyes welled up as I said this but this was a decision I was making out of love for Sammy. I didn't think he could resume his life if he had cancer. This choice, ultimately falls on many people with beloved four legged friends and as with my cat I chose for him, not for myself. I knew Sammy too well and chemo and frequent visits with the vet did not fit his spirit as I understood it. The vet looked grave. "I will look for metastasis," she said, and I felt my world tilt even more.

I moved into our new apartment on the day Sammy underwent surgery. Somehow, as I waited for the phone to ring I had an optimistic sense that he would be all right. The ultrasound had picked up fluid in with the mass and I believed cancer would not be filled with fluid. As I held that thought, the phone rang.

"The spleen came out," said my vet, "and we sent it to pathology. We won't know anything for sure until the results come back and it may take seven days." I was still optimistic. I knew it would be fine in my heart, but then I saw Sammy cut from his chest to his pelvis. The cut was stitched, of course, but was raw and red and one of the worst sights I could imagine.

Attached to an IV bag, Sammy was on morphine and looked stunned, sleepy and dazed. He stayed at the vet, sleeping most of the time in a large kennel with lots of blankets under him and my tee shirt near his nose. I wanted him to be able to smell me, know I was near. I visited him for hours every day, as did Beatriz and her husband and Michele. On the fourth day the vet nurses and I took him outside for a walk. He could barely move. He looked old, crippled and scrawny. He walked tentatively and looked awful. I was shaking. How had this terrible thing happened? Where was my dog?

Finally, on Day Seven, the pathology report declared the mass to be a benign hematoma, a huge blood blister in layman's terms, and Sammy was ready to be discharged, to a home he had never lived in. The timing was terrible. Alberto picked him up literally and figuratively, helping him into the back seat of his car and driving him the few blocks to our new apartment.

Confused and weak, Sammy walked into the lobby and entered the new space. At once he began to whimper. I had never heard this sound before. Nothing looked familiar to him. He walked from moving boxes to furniture, much of which was also new and whimpered. My heart was splitting open. How could I have taken his precious home away from him???? He stared at himself in a large mirror that hadn't yet been hanged. His expression matched mine. It said "where am I? What happened to me?"

That first night and the night after, Beatriz slept over on an inflatable bed in the living room and much to my surprise, Sammy only wanted to sleep with her. Having been cautioned by the vet not to allow Sammy to walk too much, walk up stairs or jump, I screamed when he jumped on the bed with Beatriz. But he settled in with her. I felt abandoned and unloved, concerned that he held me responsible for all the physical and emotional anguish he was feeling.

Most animal lovers will admit that even at the height of vigilance it is not always easy to decipher what a beloved animal is telling you. And it took me a few hours the following morning to realize that the painkillers we had been sent home with were inadequate to Sammy's level of pain. I flew over to the clinic to pick up additional medication and Sammy seemed to calm down.

The horrific cut on his underside sickened me every time I saw it. How could this have happened I asked myself over and over. Had someone kicked him in the belly? How long had this hematoma been there? I yearned for answers but got nothing. Spleen injuries were not uncommon in dogs I was told.

Sammy, it seemed, was also suffering from a canine version of Stockholm Syndrome and on every walk only wanted to return to the vet's office. Somehow, in the middle of our move, he now considered it to be home. I don't think he ever accepted the Riverside Drive apartment and neither did I.

We had lived on the ninth floor in my old apartment. Thunder sounded even more awful on the 15th floor and Sammy's hiding place, which we had discovered accidentally, was now also gone and I couldn't recreate it. When the first rumble came that June he ran to bathroom, then to the kitchen, where I discovered the dishwasher soothed him.

I hated the low ceilings, the beams every four feet above my head, the upstairs neighbors, lack of water, 15th floor, the openly alcoholic super, who drank from a bottle in a paper bag in front of the building every morning. The list was endless. It was a miserable place to live and I learned in the long elevator rides, no one wanted to be there. But, because many residents were living in rent controlled apartments, they suffered in silence.

Not me. I wasn't rent controlled and I was angry as hell, feeling duped and longing for my old apartment. Nothing about this new home was good. I wanted out, way out. But the management company insisted I honor my one year lease.

Ha, I thought, they didn't understand what I do for a living. I work with the press I told them in countless telephone conversations, when I could actually get through to a real person. I appeared in their office unannounced and got nowhere. So, I made good on my threat. I contacted a reporter for the *NY Times Sunday Real Estate* section. I had a story for her, I explained. I told her about my situation and suggested that people who owned apartments, but were thinking of renting instead, needed serious education. It was a check list of what to look for and what questions to ask. She liked the story. She wrote the story.

I called the management company and threatened to reveal the address if they didn't let me out of the lease. They relented and I went back to look once again in a West End Avenue building I had liked when I was searching for a rental, but in which had nothing available at the time. I had kept the super's telephone number and called him. "Yes," he told me, "In fact, a couple is moving out tomorrow. They just had a baby and the place is too small for all of them. It's a great apartment," he added. I rushed over and amidst all of their moving boxes, I found a gem. I signed a lease the next day. But, the hard part was just beginning. Healed now and trying in vain to adjust to our five month old home, Sammy would have to move again. For any dog, but especially rescued animals, moves are very hard. Home is home and I just hoped that for both our sakes, home would be wherever I was.

During the time I was preparing to move yet again, I walked Sammy to the new apartment every day, wandering the now empty space, letting him explore, smell, acclimate. We visited in the evenings after new paint had been applied, after a useless archway leading nowhere had been filled in, after a new bedroom closet had been built. We wandered the immense marble lobby, talked to the doormen, who clearly thought I was nuts appearing nightly with a rambunctious and very eager, black and white hound. I walked him to the building from various different streets. I wanted him to finally lead the way to our new home and in two weeks he did. We moved and it felt like home immediately.

The layout was great, the rooms immense and the bathroom was big and made of marble tile. There was a washer and dryer in a closet. Beatriz was in heaven. This miracle of housekeepers corralled four people to help us move and by the day's end, all the boxes except two were unpacked and everything was put away. Of course, Sammy's can opener was in one of the unpacked boxes! I didn't know where anything was! Beatriz was and continues to be the keeper of the answer to "where is?"

The *NY Times* article appeared on the front page of the section, but we were gone and true to my word, though I was quoted in the story, I did not reveal the address of the building.

CHAPTER 24

COMMUNION

It isn't easy to explain to people what I mean when I say I have communion with Sammy. But no other word suffices. We understand each other on such an instinctual level. We could be two dogs or two people, it didn't and doesn't matter. We get one another. If we were Vulcan and Dr. Spock was around, you might say we did a mind meld somewhere in our second year together and it is an extraordinary experience. In the aftermath of his splenectomy, this "one-ness," elevated to a new height.

We may not speak the same language but it isn't necessary. I adore every cell of his being. His personality seems to precede him and he is stunning in the breadth of his emotional wisdom. His behavior with children and with the elderly is always a modification of his regular Sammy self. He has patience for old people, stopping to let himself be stroked by frail, shaky hands and sometimes not so gentle fingers. A neighbor with Multiple Sclerosis once approached Sammy in the lobby and in her uncoordinated manner slapped at his head meaning to pet him, but slapping nonetheless, and he stood there allowing it. I intervened after a few seconds because though he was being a saint, I couldn't let her continue.

He seems to delight in children. He becomes one of them in a manner that is somewhat inexplicable. His demeanor changes as does his energy. Although on a particularly soggy, hot summer night we were about two blocks from home when a little boy spotted Sammy rounding the corner. My dog, I knew, was overheated and wanted to get to a bowl of water, but the child squealed in delight, "Mommy, it's a fire dog. Can I pet him, can I?" the mother looked at me, Sammy looked at me and I said yes, but when the boy's approach was too slow, Sammy barked and the child backed up. "I am so sorry," I consoled, "It's just really hot and he needs water." We moved on. A moment later I felt a tug on my shirt. It was the little, dark haired boy. "I wasn't scared you know," he said very seriously. "It was just unexpected!" I had to stop from laughing. He was so cute and indignant. "I know," I said. "He has a really loud voice." "He does," said the child and stormed off.

On an intensely cold and blustery winter night, Sammy in his warm, fleecy winter coat and me in layers of sweaters, scarves and a hat, I never wore a hat before Sammy, were half walking, half running up Broadway when Sammy stopped to observe a man in a wheelchair buying a newspaper at a corner newsstand. The man, in his forties, with a strong upper build and a head of dark hair held back in a ponytail, pushed off from the newsstand and began rolling in the same direction as we were going. I tried to pick up our pace, but Sammy fell into step with the wheelchair. The man stopped rolling and looked at me quizzically.

"Is he doing what I think he's doing?" he asked. "I think so," I replied. It seemed Sammy was keeping pace with the man. Why? I don't know. But was he doing it? Indeed. "My," exclaimed the man," He is something." "That he is," I said. He reached out to pet Sammy's head and Sammy sat. My God, what I creature I had stumbled upon.

Our communion was interesting on several levels. That it existed was a miracle, but it did not come with wild, slobbery doggy kisses and exuberant licking. I have often wondered if Sammy was born with the capacity for that or if someone had trained him not to be affectionate. I have seen dogs jump in the air in the ecstasy of the moment they see their owner. Leaps and bounds were never in Sammy's arsenal. And, yet with every fiber of my being I know how much this dog loves me. I know because yes, he is a rescue and I understand that their emotional wiring is often times different. His is different. Yet, try to separate him from me on the street and you can instantly see his bond to me. Even if it's Beatriz. If the leash passes from me to someone else and I go in another direction, he becomes frantic to get to me. He will gladly leave me behind in the apartment and go for a walk with someone else, but try to wrest his leash away on the street and it's a whole different story.

We visited a friend of mine one day and I got up to go to the bathroom. When I came out my friend said, somewhat in wonder, "My god, the moment you closed the door he went and sat in front of it. I have never seen that before." Truth be told, even at home, closed doors are not welcome. Sammy needs egress to everywhere, all the time. He needs access to me. And, then he usually ignores me. Go figure, it's a little bit like my marriage was!

I watch Sammy interact with his walker friends and he licks their hands, sometimes, though rarely, their faces. Me? Not so much! I often joke that I am "food lady," the bearer of all sorts of goodies, hence his happiness at seeing me, but in my heart I know otherwise. Love is love, no matter how it's expressed and I am not a mushy type of person either, but I love to put my hand on him gently as he sleeps on my bed beside me. I love the comfort and knowledge of him in my life.

CHAPTER 25

STARRY, STARRY NIGHT

In July of Sammy's tenth year I decided that I needed a vacation. I hadn't had one in several years and Beatriz was heading back to Colombia to visit her family. I scheduled my time away to coincide with hers.

What I longed for was simple. I wanted to rent a small cottage, without a lot of people around me and I wanted to bring Sammy along. So I looked on the Internet until I found five potential spots. Three wouldn't let me bring a dog. Of the other two, one sounded truly ideal. Attached to a Bed & Breakfast that also hosted a four star restaurant on the premises, it bordered the Delaware River on the Pennsylvania side and was also flanked by what sounded historical, the Delaware Canal, which in truth turned out to be an algae covered, stagnant strip of water that ran about twenty feet away from the cottage. Our little home had two entrances, one from the road side and one from the canal side. The road side required walking up about ten steps. The canal side featured a delightful veranda with two tables, umbrellas and a rustic wooden fence. I was in love! It was perfect for us.

The Innkeeper was a bit unwelcoming, surly to be truthful, and announced that she also had a dog, a pug, so we should coordinate schedules to make sure our walks didn't coincide. Strange, I thought, until I encountered her snarling, territorial, feisty little animal. Walk on my path, will you? It seemed to challenge Sammy and me. We tried to steer clear.

Our accommodations were a little challenging at first. The bedroom featured an enormously high canopy bed and it sported a little step stool, because even humans would have a problem getting up on it. Sammy would surely never have been able to and so we opted to sleep on the convertible sofa in the living room. To say the mattress was less than stellar would be a gross mis-statement of the facts. It was horrible with every spring and coil poking through to aggravate the best of backs and mine surely wasn't among the best.

I had brought along Sammy's bed, his food, which was frozen hamburger, only to discover the kitchen had everything except a refrigerator. I knew from early queries that it didn't have a stove. A toaster, microwave oven and sink, along with plates and cutlery were in evidence, but nothing for cooking. Of course, because they wanted everyone to eat in the restaurant!! But, we had come prepared. I had smuggled in an electric hot plate on which to cook Sammy's food, hoping no one would smell the burgers sizzling. I spied a mini bar and pried it open, revealing a chilly interior. I piled the hamburgers in there figuring I would use them until they all thawed and then buy some fresh ground meat.

I had brought toys and everything I could think to make our temporary home, homey. Intrigued by the new surroundings Sammy quickly pried me away from unpacking to explore. There were unfamiliar greens growing here we discovered and one made him sneeze. I asked one of the Inn's staff what it was and she informed me it was "stinkweed." "Is there any other vegetation I should know about," I asked. "Oh yeah, there's some poison ivy, but I haven't seen much of that yet this summer and it's August already."

No stove, stinkweed and maybe poison ivy. I mused, were we on vacation or camping, albeit in very pricey digs? But Sammy was joyful. The reddish colored, dirt path that ran along the canal was about four feet wide and seemed endless. To our left I spotted a small bridge and under it the path veered off to the left and out of view. To our right the path seemed to go on for miles. It turned out to be two and half to be precise and it became our morning walk.

Also to the left was what appeared to be a garden for rocking in a swinging chaise and just contemplating the peace, broken only by the vroom of motorcycles. Yes, even here in Eden, on the week-ends motorcyclists abounded and broke the peace. But, it was generally quiet. A giant ceramic white horse guarded the gate to the garden and when he first encountered it Sammy began barking wildly. He had never seen a dog this size he seemed to be saying, until he smelled it and decided, dog, it was not. No sense barking if it couldn't respond.

That night after I cooked Sammy's hamburger and ordered in dinner from the restaurant, we began to relax. And, may I say that relaxing is not always all it is cracked up to be. There was nothing to do. Every time I turned on the TV that had virtually no reception, or plugged ear buds in my ears to listen to an audiobook, Sammy looked at me with a "So, what are we supposed to do next?" expression. We were not living in a mansion and he had already explored every crevice, so I grabbed my flashlight and little, attachable-to-your clothes, insect repellant and we headed out for our first night walk.

Two things happened right away, the insect repellant fell off of my waistband and rolled to who knows where and I discovered my lovely little flashlight barely illuminated one step ahead of us. It was pitch black outside, deep, dense, cut it with a knife black. The hum and buzz of insects droned around us. Undaunted, though really scared, I kept assuring myself that I was a New York City girl and would handle whatever might come, but there was forest all around us and I didn't know exactly what might be coming. Freddy Kruger came to mind, as well as black bears. I had no idea what was waiting for us under the little bridge. The flashlight was trained on Sammy so he could see where he was and I followed. Need a bigger flashlight I reminded myself for the next day. Actually a floodlight would have been perfect. And so we walked, I got bitten by everything flitting past me in the dark and Sammy sneezed a lot. No poop. None to be sniffed, scarfed or deposited. We're going back I thought as I picked up our pace.

Once safely in the cottage I made up the creaky, squeaky convertible and Sammy jumped on it and glared at me. "This is where we're supposed to sleep?" he seemed to be accusing me. But, dutifully he lay down in the middle of the mattress and I coiled myself around him and somehow we slept. I loved cuddling him as he never permitted this behavior at home.

The next morning, at six to be precise, Sammy bounded off the bed turned to me with excitement and a face that said "Move it lady. Let's go." I threw on open toed comfy shoes and a hoody and opened the door to a brilliant August morning. It was freezing cold!!! Invigorated and well-slept, my joyful dog pulled me to the right and off we went. I pulled up the hood. It was so cold! The dirt from the path immediately went into my shoes. My nose began to run, but Sammy was gleefully looking for other dog's left behinds, smells to mark and pee on, but there were none. Apparently the pugnacious little pug who lived in the Inn didn't go this far.

All at once Sammy stopped dead in his tracks assuming a Pointer-like stance, with one leg bent and his tail straight out behind him. I followed his gaze and saw two graceful deer with plume-like, curled up white tails leaping over the canal and into the woods. Sammy looked up at me with wonder. City folk that we were, deer were not in our vocabulary. "They're deer," I explained to Sammy and he seemed to understand some part of this, it was okay, he was reassured and pulled in their direction. What would they make with the likes of him I thought. But, they were gone.

I discovered a few things quickly. On this old path I didn't need to be my City self, so I shucked my bra, forgot about styling my hair and wandered around that morning. I didn't care what anyone at the Inn thought. This, I thought was a vacation!!!! Midday we wandered to the left and explored a new path. It led as it turned out directly to the Delaware river. Sadly, we saw a deer carcass that Sammy instinctively avoided and we went to the river's edge. I could almost hear my dog think "Wow, this is one big puddle." He tentatively put a foot in, then two. The river had a strong current, so I wasn't inclined to literally test the waters to learn if I also had a "water dog." Knee deep in the water I was forced to guide Sammy back out, but he lapped at the moving current nonetheless and we made our way over to several large rocks resting at the river's edge. One was big and flat and I sat and so did Sammy. We gazed around at a serene, unblemished bright blue sky and trees that resembled animals. I named one Giraffe Tree and a rock that jutted out of the water became Hippo Rock. It was so still and magnificent. Just what my soul needed. Our rock became Meditation Rock for it seemed Sammy was in a Zen frame of mind as well.

That night, we shared what may turn out to be one of the most wonderful memories of my life. Always celestially oriented, but very city-bound, I longed with a deep intensity to see a shooting star. Not a run of the mill distant streak in the sky, though that would have sufficed as well, but the real deal. I had seen them in movies and once while traveling to Texas in November had been promised an amazing meteorite shower, which I planned to watch from my airplane window, but I never saw even one streak.

Sammy and I had drifted into a quiet silence after dinner that night, our illicit hamburger smell hopefully long dissipated. I missed our regular walking time by about twenty minutes and my pup didn't seem to have a sense of urgency about him, so I relaxed for another twenty minutes. If Freddy Kruger was waiting for me, he would just have to wait, I thought. Finally, we were ready to go. And, I can't exactly explain what happened in the next five minutes.

We crossed the veranda with its rusty little gate and stepped out on the path. I looked down ahead of me, and then unexpectedly looked up at the sky. This was not my habit, because with the intense darkness I had learned to rely exclusively on my, by now, bigger and better, flashlight. The trees on either side of the canal drifted towards one another overhead, but left an open expanse between them and as I looked into this open patch of black sky, I spotted a glorious, brilliant streak of light splitting the sky in a high arc, just visible through this cut-out in the foliage. It was my shooting star, I registered in utter amazement, as it arched directly above me and I could swear I heard it sizzle as it was engulfed in the rich blackness. Had I not looked up, or walked as late as I did, I would have never seen it.

I was so excited and exhilarated I whooped for joy and Sammy, not understanding the shooting star, but catching my euphoria, did his own little, twirly happy dance on the canal path. This kind of event might have had nowhere nearly as much significance for most people, other than to say it was beautiful. But, I had waited a lifetime to see exactly this. It may be the only shooting star I will ever see in my life, and if so then it will have been enough. At times if I am very tense or stressed, I sometimes think of this beautiful celestial messenger and I am centered in the universe as I was that night. When I say I have shared some of the happiest moments of my life with my dear dog, I usually think of this brief encounter with the heavens and I am so grateful he was there to share it with me.

On this trip, I took many photographs of Sammy with a camera, not my cellphone, and captured some of the more special moments of our vacation. One picture in particular stood out from the others. Sammy and I had been heading down the path next to the canal one afternoon and I felt safe enough to drop his leash to allow me to photograph him. He walked a few steps ahead not realizing he was "free," and suddenly stopped, looked at the leash on the ground and then looked at me with an expression that was at once concerned and seemed to ask "aren't you coming?" I snapped the picture in that instant and when the picture was developed I was struck by its unintentional composition. Behind Sammy, the dusty, red clay trail narrowed off into the distance and on either side was a wild rush of lush, green vegetation, with purple and yellow flowers poking through. Between us on the path was the dropped leash and his expression that told me he wanted to be attached; to go where he chose, but to know I was simply attached.

I had the picture enlarged, vowing to frame it. When I looked at it though, sadness flooded my view. I thought to myself, "One day you will need to walk this path without me Sweetheart and I hope my mother is there to meet you where the path ends." It was a sorrowful thought and perhaps the reason that I waited years to have it framed. The dropped leash tells such a deep story with his expression and it hurt to look at it for too long.

CHAPTER 26

GOTTA' RUN

While we were away we had been blessed with extraordinary clear, blue sky-filled days, but August that summer was a very stormy one and when we returned to Manhattan it caught us up in a whirlwind of thunder and flash-bomb lightening. Sometimes the earth felt as if it would split open.

Sammy ran for cover, but now in our relatively new apartment we had to find a new hiding place. It was hard to find. The moment a rain drop fell, Sammy was off and running. He had become so sensitized to the sound of the impending storm that he wasted no time, but no space seemed to offer shelter. So I sat on the floor with him, draping his trembling body with a towel from nose to snout and waited out the storm. I considered myself fortunate in that as he got older he no longer thought the storm was in our apartment. Maybe we had had too many apartments for that old thinking to prevail!

One evening, Michele was walking him at 5 PM. She arrived home breathless with Sammy in tow.

"Sammy got out of his leash," she exclaimed, trying to regain her breath. "We were walking in the park and a kid jumped on a big, dead tree branch lying on the path and Sammy must have thought it was thunder because he ran across Riverside Drive and I thought he was going to get hit by a car." She barely paused to inhale. "He ran all the way up 85th street until he came to the front door of the building. I was so relieved that it was open because I didn't catch up with him until he was at the back elevator."

She eyed me quizzically. "Why are you so calm?" she asked.

"Because he's here," I said, "Simply because he's here."

But, Sammy didn't stop this runaway dog routine having learned how to slip backwards out of his collar and bolt. It was how I had almost lost him in the rain years before. I begrudgingly tightened his collar. I deliberately kept it a little looser because of a quirk I had. I hated to have him in a collar, though truthfully, it was the best way to help prevent his poop eating. To me it felt as if I was enslaving him and I didn't want to choke him. But in his best interest I made it more snug. I also bought a slip collar; a small piece of chain that would automatically tighten if he strained against it in either direction. I gave it to whoever was walking him if there was even a threat of rain. I obligingly put it in my pocket as well because I never wanted a repeat incident of what we had gone through.

Sammy was of a different mind though and having learned how to slip backwards to freedom, he began to practice this routine even when the sun was shining. So, it became of matter of asking him, "Which way do you want to go," when approaching an intersection or quite literally, an impasse, meaning I, or a walker, wanted to go one way and he wanted to go another. A stranger on the street, watching this little act one day suggested to me that when Sammy wouldn't go my way, I walk him around in a complete circle and it would confuse him. Interesting, I thought, and tried it and it worked. Once. Everyone tried it to find it worked once. But, Sammy was going to outwit us all. It was very scary because a couple of times it happened while crossing the street.

So, in the end, Sammy got his way. It was his walk after all, I thought, why not let him make some of the decisions. It seemed he made them at every street corner, having four different paths he could select from. "Which way do you want to go?" became part of our dialogue. I watched other people yank their dogs this way and that and thought that walking one's dog should not be mixed together with running errands. It was their time to enjoy being out and in the best of circumstances good bonding time for us.

Retraining my thinking was not a new thing for me by now. My darling dog had retrained virtually everything I once held to be true. He, it turns out, had truly trained me!!!

CHAPTER 27

NEW NEIGHBORS??

Though we had only moved four blocks in our most recent move, we inherited an entirely new cast of neighbors both on our floor and on the street.

I began to call a group of dogs who I spotted on my early evening walks *The Old Dog Parade.* With slow gaits and sometimes wobbly legs and almost always with white fur around their noses and mouths, they came in all sizes and breeds. I marveled at the calm and patience of the owners. They were rarely composed of the men and women who could not be pried off their cell phones, even to watch their own children. I wondered if we would one day join this parade.

With daylight savings time that fall, Sammy began to wake earlier and earlier.

"You're walking your dog at what time?" asked my friend, Rachel.

"5:30 in the morning," I said balefully, already expecting the zero understanding or sympathy I would get. But instead, Rachel said, "So when do you put on makeup?"

"I don't." I laughed. "Who's looking at me at 5:30 in the morning? If there's anyone on the street besides doormen, I'm just a sleepy looking middle aged woman with a black and white hound," I said.

"I couldn't do that," Rachel remarked. "What about your hair?

"Honestly, I don't care," I replied. "Really, no one is looking anymore. I've become invisible. It's okay."

On one of my very early morning Sammy walks I flashed back to a memory of my mother recounting how, as a young woman, newly arrived in Paris, with my father and two year old me, she had gone out wearing a red "chapeau." Her hat must have been a real attention getter because men whistled and admired her all the way to the store and back. She had always smiled when she told the story. She remembered her "pretty" days so fondly.

My red chapeau days had apparently been laid to rest as I realized, not for the first time, how little male attention I got lately, or had not been getting for almost a decade now. My Hungarian genes had kept my skin looking good without the benefit of cosmetic procedures, but men knew middle aged when they saw it and when they saw it, their interest vaporized. Why was it so okay I wondered not for the first time? When had it become okay to be invisible?

It was easy to remember when men followed me on the street and a man driving a tiny car in Rome had driven up on the sidewalk to flirt. But, I was slow to realize how infrequently this happened after my divorce. I recalled a discussion between Zsa Zsa Gabor and the character actress, Hermione Gingold, on television a long time ago. Perhaps in their early fifties, Hermione had reached over and patted Zsa Zsa solicitously on the knee, saying "I feel sorry for you my dear." Clearly offended, Zsa Zsa had glared at her. "You've always been beautiful," continued the other actress, "and as you age you will mourn the loss of that beauty. I have never been beautiful. And, I seem to be getting better looking with age."

She was right, I thought, it was a loss. But, shouldn't I be fighting back more? Maybe not with online dating, I thought, but how?

I remembered my mother again, who had never lied about her age or even contemplated the face lift that was the middle aged rite of passage for all her Hungarian friends. When, I wondered had I become so like my mother?

So, as it happened one early morning, I was staring up at the perfect globe of a full moon over Riverside Park. Half naked trees moved softly in the early fall chill. I was still half asleep with my very awake dog, when I practically bumped into a man heading toward me trailed by a small long haired dachshund.

"Sorry I startled you," he apologized. "Getting old, huh?"

"Excuse me?" I glowered. "I am still half asleep, but nice to see that there are rude people on the street at all times of the day and night!"

He seemed perplexed and then laughed. "I meant your dog," he said and grinned. "Mine too. Fourteen next month."

Gaining my bitchy balance, which seemed often to be my style lately, I grinned back. "It's so difficult to know which one of us is older these days," I said by way of apology. "It's tough, isn't it?" he asked.

"Him getting old, or me?" I asked. "Him," he said as he appeared to appraise me. "For five in the morning you look pretty good to me!"

I fell completely silent. It had been so long that anyone had flirted with me, I was at loss for words. Was he flirting I wondered. "Oh," was all I could muster and then not knowing what else to say, I moved away. "Duty calls," I said pointing to Sammy, who was totally still "Why," I thought to myself, "why aren't you pulling me down the street the way you usually do when I try to speak to someone. Now, when I need rescuing, you're just standing there?" As if in some telepathic response, Sammy began tugging me away.

"You're never going to believe this," I said to my best friend Anne, who had long ago predicted that I would meet a new man because of Sammy. I told her about the early morning encounter, which was growing dimmer by the minute. "Honestly, it was so early and I was asleep on my feet. I didn't know what to say. How do you make conversation before the crack of dawn with a total stranger?"

"Were you wearing makeup?" Rachel asked, when I also told her about my brief meeting.

"Again, I repeat, are you nuts? No one wears makeup at that hour of the morning. I would fall asleep at the sink." "Will you wear some tomorrow morning?" she queried. "No," I said. But, I thought to myself, should I put on a little something? I discounted the idea immediately. "I have never seen this man before and probably never will again. I am lucky if I run a brush through my hair and really that's only for the doorman, so he doesn't think I am a lunatic attached to a leash," I said.

Rachel laughed. "You'll be sorry."

How prophetic I thought as I saw the small dachshund heading toward me the next morning.

"Hey," said the man who I realized was a little taller than me. Was it the same man? I began taking in the details I had missed the morning before. Brown hair, a bit shaggy, but it was all there, still. Or was it a toupee, I wondered and then thought, who would bother to put on a toupee to walk their dog at five in the morning? No, but it wasn't a piece, I realized, just nice hair. He wore a black and grey checked flannel shirt, out, over jeans.

"What's your dog's name?" I asked.

"Annabelle," he said a little sheepishly. "My daughter named her."

Oh, he's married, of course, I thought. He looked a little too old to have a daughter living at home, but it was probably a second or even third marriage; quite common in Manhattan. Anticipation, that I hadn't known I had, evaporated suddenly, blending into the grey tones of the emerging morning. "Well, nice to bump into you and Annabelle, "I murmured and walked away.

I called Anne several hours later. "Crap," I spit out the word. "Crap. It was so nice to live in content oblivion. I cannot believe I hoped I'd see him again and he's married." "What's his name?" asked Anne.

"Annabelle," I said, catching myself, "that's the dog's name. I never got as far as his name. You have to know the dog comes with a daughter! What on earth was I thinking? His wife is probably fast asleep in their co-op, with their teenage daughter in the next room and here I am thinking I should have worn makeup."

"Maybe you should have," said Rachel when I told her the story. "You never know." Maybe he's not married," she added.

But, I never saw him or Annabelle again. It wasn't until much later that it occurred to me that perhaps I had not seen them again because Annabelle had died. It was a terribly sad thought. I looked at Sammy. Was he getting old enough for people to think he was an older dog? He looked the same to me. But, then again, I looked the same to me. What did I know?

CHAPTER 28

THE POWER OF CHEERIOS

Throughout most of my life I have watched people walking their dogs and I have watched the dogs, not all, but many, gaze up with love at the person walking next to them. I have always thought this was adoration. But, I was wrong! It was all about treats!!! Who knew?

Until Sammy was introduced to Cheerios and until I made the decision that carrying a few Cheerios in my pocket was a good idea to persuade Sammy to go in the direction I had in mind, I never understood the power they held.

On our walks Sammy had infrequently looked up at me from four paces ahead to make sure, I guess, that I was still tethered to his leash. But, he never looked up at me in unabashed adoration . . . . until the ubiquitous breakfast cereal became part of our lives. From the moment I gave Sammy a tiny oat circle to avoid having to tug on his leash, my dog starred up at me as if I was the eighth wonder of the world. People would pass us on the street and say "Aw, look at him, he loves you so much," but I knew otherwise. He was hoping for another Cheerio. It got so that I was carrying more than a few and we would do what I called "The Cheerio two step, take two steps, look up at me, take another two, look up again." As people misinterpreted this behavior, I would smile and say, "No, it's not love, it's Cheerios!"

One day I passed a group of hungry looking pigeons. It was cold outside and not much food had been tossed to the street, so I flung a fistful of Cheerios in their direction. Sammy glowered at me! Glowered. "It's okay", I reassured him, "there's plenty for all of you," but he wasn't convinced.

From the first Cheerio, I began to observe and understand the behavior of dogs I passed on the street. Most of the time, the person walking the dog seemed unaware of the starring, or maybe they were ignoring it, but I was amused. It was a secret only dog owners would really share!

Cheerios became a morning routine in our apartment as well. Every day, after I showered, Sammy would wait for me in the hallway outside the bathroom. Occasionally he pushed his nose in, if not to rush me along, but because he didn't want a closed door between us. When I finally emerged, we would head into the living room where Beatriz sat with a quarter of a cup of Cheerios and we would begin our Cheerio dance. He would stand between her legs and almost inhale the Cheerios from her hand. One at time wasn't fast enough and in Spanish Beatriz would tell him to "espire," – breathe. A particularly charming video that I captured on my phone had Sammy pushing her hand with his nose. "Faster, faster," he seemed to be saying and at one point, Beatriz, in her haste, dropped a Cheerio. Sammy stepped back and barked at her twice. "Yes, yes, it's yours. I know," she said and he plunged forward for more. Even as Sammy got older and couldn't really stand for long periods, this routine persisted, sometimes with Beatriz kneeling in front of him while he lay on the floor.

In her absence, if she was sick or on vacation, I became the provider of the tiny oats, but never seemed to create the same high-energy scenario as Beatriz. Not that Sammy didn't eat the Cheerios, but it wasn't with the same "game-playing" enthusiasm he mustered for his second Mom. She had a natural, playful energy that seemed to inspire him.

CHAPTER 27

OLD DOG VESTIBULAR EAR, AND . . .

I was watching television one evening with Sammy snoozing on my bed, when I noticed him look up very suddenly and swing his head from side to side. His eyes were wild. Even in his worst thunder storm moment I had never seen this before. I wrapped my hands around his head to stabilize him all the while semi screaming, "Sammy, Sammy." I was wild with fear. What was happening to him? Was it a stroke, a seizure. I didn't seem able to connect with him. He wouldn't stop the wild gyrations. Finally, after a few minutes, they began to subside and he began to pant. If anything he was as frightened as me.

My dog walker, Edwin, who had been a doorman at my old co-op, arrived just at that moment, took in the scene of my clutching a panting Sammy, and said "what happened? What's wrong?" I began to weep. "I don't know," I sobbed as I tried to get my hands to stop shaking. "I need to call the vet."

When I described Sammy's symptoms, she counseled me to calm down and bring him in the next day. "If it has stopped completely," she said, "it might be Old Dog Vestibular Ear syndrome."

His eye movements were apparently called nystagmus. "It happens sometimes as they get older," she said.

There it was again. Sammy was ten and I was stunned to think of him as older. We had only had five years together thus far. This wasn't possible, I thought. My vet assured me that Sammy was in great shape and not an old dog, but a mature one and this syndrome did develop with age and was an inner ear disturbance. She suggested I get a neurologic consult to be on the safe side and recommended a neurologist at a larger animal medical center. I made an appointment. Beatriz came with me. I was terrified of what he might find.

The neuro vet was a man in his 40's who exuded a sense of quiet. He examined Sammy with Beatriz and me present in the exam room. With a nurse he skillfully turned Sammy in many directions and using a foam cradle placed Sammy on his back, legs up. I resisted the urge to rescue my dog, but he seemed to be compliant, whereas I felt frantic. Using treats to guide Sammy's eyes, the vet tested virtually every part of him. He examined his spine, his tail, his ears. When he was finished, he said "Okay, he seems to be fine and I would concur that this probably is Old Dog Vestibular Ear, but if you want, we can perform an MRI to rule out a tumor."

It is so important to ask the right questions at moments like this, so you can make informed decisions. "How will he hold still for an MRI?" I asked, thinking of the ones I had had and the noise they made. "He would be sedated," said the vet. "How?" I asked. "With general anesthesia," he responded. "What is the risk?" I asked. "With anesthesia there is always a risk and he will need to be under for an hour and a half." I have never been a big fan of anesthesia for myself or Sammy. "If you find a tumor what would be the next step?" "That's up to you," said the vet. "He is in otherwise good health so I would remove the tumor."

My God, brain surgery? "How long will the effects of the anesthesia last?" I asked. "About three days, maybe a little grogginess, maybe a little diarrhea."

This, oddly, was not a tough decision for me. We had survived his splenectomy. I wasn't letting anyone slice into Sammy's brain. No MRI, no anything, I decided. I wasn't going to put him through that.

Through the next few years, we have experienced several bouts of Old Dog Vestibular Ear and each presented somewhat differently, so sometimes it took me awhile to realize what it was. Because Sammy had been asleep on my bed the first time, I never saw him sag to the floor, lose his balance or any of the side effects of this syndrome. But, they were in evidence each subsequent time he had a bout.

What did happen within days of our neuro consult was bizarre and frightening. Sammy didn't have another episode, rather he walked towards me from the foyer and as I watched a line of urine formed behind him. He wasn't marking or urinating, but a ten foot stream of pee formed behind him. "What the hell?" I thought. He seemed completely unaware. It happened again the next day. I recalled that the vet had said when exploring Sammy's spine that he might have a herniated disk in his lower back at the L5 vertebrae. I had this as well, courtesy of lifting my sweet dog when he injured his leg and I knew for some people this herniation could result in incontinence.

I called the neuro guy and asked "When you pushed on Sammy's spine is it possible you put too much pressure on his L5 vertebrae?" To his credit, he didn't rush to deny the possibility and acknowledged that this type of herniation could cause incontinence, but it would be unusual he explained.

As it happened we had a newcomer to our little group of Sammy caregivers and her name was Lidia. She saw him urinate unexpectedly in the dining room, a few days later and was very surprised. "I don't think he's doing this deliberately," I told her. The next day Lidia came home from a Sammy walk with a terrified expression on her face. "He's bleeding, Suzanne. Sammy is bleeding when he pees."

It was the dead of a very cold winter and we had had a large snowstorm after our visit with the neuro vet and there were mounds of snow everywhere. The blood showed up instantly and Lidia was beyond concerned. "We have to get him to the vet," I mustered and called to let them know we were coming. Sammy lifted his leg to pee every ten feet or so and each time, bright red blood spurted out on the snow. It was an awful sight.

My poor, sweet dog had to stay at the vet until they determined he had an e-Coli bacterial infection in his bladder and the bladder had formed so many crystals, they were literally cutting him and causing the bleeding. Over three days they treated him with IV antibiotics and then we came home. He was still bleeding, but not as much, but seemed a little disoriented. In retrospect, they probably released him too early and without pain medication.

When we entered the apartment, he walked around as if in unfamiliar surroundings making a sound I had only heard once before when a cow at a farm camp I had attended as child, had given birth. It was lowing sound, deep and terrible and as he went from room to room it became mixed with a whimper. This I recognized at once. He was in pain. I still had some pain medication from his splenectomy and without further thought immediately gave him a dose. Then I called the vet who approved my decision! Why hadn't this been their decision upon releasing him I wondered, angry and concerned.

The infection took several more days to resolve and the bleeding, even though faint, was still visible against the snow and broke my heart, until finally it stopped. I couldn't help examining the snow however for weeks to come.

CHAPTER 29

PLANETS IN OUR BACKYARD

Thank heaven, the planets seemed to align well for us as winter turned to spring and as the frigid winter winds subsided. Sammy and I began walking along Riverside Drive, which, as in its name, snakes along the Hudson River.

In the early evening sky one day I looked over the river's horizon and was stunned to see an early crescent moon flanked by two enormous bright spheres of light. The view was spectacular and though Sammy had other business to attend to, I stood transfixed at this celestial finery. What was it, I wondered. A quick check online revealed that Venus and Saturn had formed this astronomical piece of artwork and it lasted for weeks.

I took to pointing it out to total strangers on the street. Look up, I told passers-by. Most took well to my intrusion on what seemed to be their end of the day trek home. Others, not so much. I didn't really care. I would have been thrilled if someone had shown this array to me and more so to learn these were planets. Mars rose high in the night sky that year too, so I dragged my doorman out to see it with the faint red glow that defines this planet. He seemed to appreciate my enthusiasm, because I had such an urge to share this bounty. It lifted my spirits in the way few Earth-bound things can!

This viewing made me long for a country vacation again and I began to scour the internet for dog-friendly nearby vacation spots. This time we wound up in Tannersville, New York and I knew we were in trouble when I spied people wearing sweatshirts that read "Welcome to Bear Country." Two and a half hours outside of New York and up a very big mountain, Tannersville wasn't much of a town, having fallen on very hard times when the economy crashed. We were staying in a lovely Inn and once again had our own cottage, again with a veranda, but this one had a roof, so we could sit outside even when it rained. I had breakfast in this peaceful setting every morning and Sammy placidly snoozed by my chair. We both seemed to crave a break from the noise of the city, at least I did.

I had brought all the requisite paraphernalia with me and they had graciously dropped the bed down to the floor so Sammy had easy access, but the moment the sun went down we could hear coyotes in surround sound. Even Sammy looked a bit undone. Where were we?

The Inn kept lights on, when they remembered, to illuminate the area outside the main building, but still if we moved out of the perimeter, we met with pitch blackness and the baying of coyotes was extraordinary. Relaxed I wasn't. Nor was I seeing stars because I was too afraid to look up and take my eyes away from what might be approaching.

One morning in our meandering walk we stumbled across what I can only imagine was bear dung. Sammy eyed it. Poop this was not, he seemed to surmise and I wondered about the size of what would have left such a pile.

We both became bored quickly. We went into town, but there was nothing much to sniff or buy. A shop owner told me that she believed her small dog, who had been left out in her backyard had been snatched by a coyote. She bent to pet Sammy. "Be careful," she said. I was and home we went after four days. It was a nice idea in theory, but the execution was lacking in peace. I have not seen another shooting star!

CHAPTER 30

ANOTHER SCARE!!!

We had been experiencing a calm that history had taught me could be shattered at any time and sure enough that fall, Sammy was about to go to sleep when he bolted for the foyer. I followed anxiously to find him heaving and then vomiting. For some inexplicable reason known only to him, Sammy vomited only in the foyer, on the few occasions that he needed to do this.

He kept vomiting until all he brought up was white foam and bile. I grabbed the phone and as I had done on several occasions in the past years, told the overnight nurse that we were in trouble. She counseled me to watch him and wait until morning to bring him in. Bad advice. I knew once again we were in trouble. Sammy looked exhausted, but periodically kept heaving up foam. I was in touch with the nurse throughout the night. My poor sick Sammy managed to get to his water bowl but on the way had diarrhea. I cleaned it up, shaky now, called the nurse again. Same advice. I should have been firmer about getting him seen then, not in the morning.

I wrapped a blanket around me and lay down on the sofa to keep vigil. I must have dozed off because when I woke, I saw Sammy, flat as a pancake, diarrhea behind him and I knew I had to take action immediately. For some reason, perhaps because of Sammy's history, I had kept the telephone number for a pet ambulance near my phone. I called them only to learn it might take an hour to get to us. "Hurry," I pleaded as I couldn't lift Sammy and carry him to a taxi. He was dead weight.

I called Beatriz, who arrived at the same time as the ambulance tech. He brought with him, not a gurney as I expected but a large green flat canvas apparatus. He gingerly moved Sammy on to this thing that turned out to be a duffle carrier of some sort and I called the vet – it was 6:30 in the morning. The duffle carrying my dog was put on a gurney and lifted into the ambulance, the first, and thankfully, only one I have ever been in. The ride was bumpy and only lasted five minutes, but in that time, with Sammy strapped to the gurney and Beatriz clutching my hand, we were both brimming with tears.

A team met us at the front door to the clinic and Sammy was "triaged" with x-rays, bloodwork and I am not certain what else. He was so sick he couldn't lift his head and for once, he didn't make eye contact with me. IV fluids were inserted into his arm and the vet called for an ultrasound.

In short order it was determined that he had something more commonly found in cats, called cholangiohepatitis. Bacteria from his intestines had spurted up into his liver effectively shutting it down. His liver enzymes had sky rocketed and he needed massive doses of antibiotics by IV. He couldn't eat solid food for three days. Again, we all took to visiting him, me for hours on end. He was listless and drained of energy. He would recover I was assured, but looking at him I had a problem believing this.

On the fourth day I was encouraged to bring him food and feed him by hand. By then, my disgust with canned, processed dog food, had propelled me to a canine nutritionist and Sammy's diet now consisted of ground turkey breast, mixed with garbanzo beans, a vitamin supplement powder and Cheerios as treats. He had been thriving on this diet for a year already and I cooked a fresh batch for him every night. So, I cooked a fresh batch and took it to the vet where to my surprise he ate, slowly, but nonetheless he ate and importantly, he kept it down.

On the fifth day we came home by "pet chauffer," a taxi service for pets and Beatriz once again stayed with me for two days and nights. She went home to New Jersey to get her husband and dog settled for the next two days and while she was gone I was alone with Sammy. He was exhausted and had lost so much muscle tone that he couldn't raise and lower his head to lie down. When he tried his entire body began to shake from the effort. It was horrific, but he was home and with piles of antibiotics, which, as it turned out, taken by mouth, caused nausea and vomiting, so we needed to get a nurse from the clinic to come to us and give him shots twice daily for ten days. Sammy turned the corner, but it was a big corner and between his panting from the slightest exertion and me crying and Beatriz and I not sleeping, it was an exhausting ordeal. Again, a lesson in not waiting. There had been no warning signs.

CHAPTER 31

WE MEET SANDRA!!!

One problem we encountered in recovery was that the nurse who was giving injections of antibiotics to Sammy twice a day had no skill and within four days his back looked like he had been crossed with an Australian Catahoula, a Pit Bull and a crocodile, There were lumps and bumps everywhere.

So, I requested a new nurse and we met Sandra, who has in every way, over three years, turned out to be a life saver and the person who can best allay my worst fears when it comes to Sammy. She listens, understands that I am, in fact, a great observer, and she instinctually knows when to placate me and when to take action. She is also a master with a syringe; giving medication, drawing blood, taking urine samples and just about everything else.

Sandra speaks to Sammy directly. She doesn't speak in baby talk, rather a sort of cartoon character voice, which he responds to with pleasure and rapt attention. I understand from her that they have conversations on the street, apparently to the delight of passersby, and she protects my sweet dog, who, with encroaching old age, needs protection as he zig zags down the street. Sandra knows Sammy does not take well to "approaches from the rear," and holds out a strong arm to stop any human or dog inclined in that direction. Really, who would welcome an unanticipated nose in the butt? Not Sammy!

Skilled to a degree not often found among veterinary nurses, Sandra's calm is contagious. While she and Sammy commune she gives me time to catch my breath emotionally, because Sammy's bout with hepatitis unhinged me. As a result of it we get bloodwork around three times a year to watch Sammy's liver enzymes. On the few occasions that they've been slightly to moderately elevated, with my vet's consent, Sammy get injections of penicillin, so we never again approach the insane liver values he had when he developed hepatitis.

Sandra is a sane voice that can penetrate my occasional bouts of Sammy insanity. When you share your life with a basically healthy dog, who frequently "gets things," you are never fully peaceful and from my experience, nor should you be. The few indicators we have, mood, quality of poop, urine and behavior need to be monitored. I learned through the years that slight changes in any of these can escalate rapidly. So, I don't wait.

Poor Sandra has spent many a night peeling me off the ceiling via texts, calming me, chiding me, coaxing me to believe "it's nothing. Don't be worried." Yet, worried I am every day because as with Old Dog Vestibular Ear syndrome, Sammy has moments in which he's fine one minute and listing over in the next.

Several summers ago on a quiet, dry evening, we went out for a walk. It was a Sunday, close to 7 PM and the streets were fairly empty. It was a lolling around kind of early evening. As we walked, Sammy leading the way, I thought I saw him list slightly to the left. Nah, I told myself, when he listed more and as I drew up beside him, he collapsed slowly against my legs, sitting on my feet.

I have never known if in a pinch I can scream, but I learned in that moment, that not only can I, I did, at the top of my lungs because no one was on the street, not even a doorman. Suddenly a middle aged couple rounded the corner and saw me. The woman rushed to my side. "What happened?" she asked, looking at my crumpled dog. "I don't know," I said, shaking, "I need to call my vet, but I don't have my cell."

This wonderful stranger whipped out her phone and handed it to me, but I had my little "Sammy-walking pouch" which held a supply of baggies, Cheerios and wipes in one hand and as I reached for her phone the pouch dropped with Cheerios spilling all over the street. My hands were shaking so hard. She dialed the number for me and I sobbed into her phone to the vet receptionist "Sammy collapsed on West End Avenue. I need help, please."

The receptionist put me on hold while she found a doctor. The stranger spoke to her husband and he left, but she stayed with me while I waited. A nurse came on the phone and asked me if he was conscious. "Yes," I said, "he just looks dazed." "Can you get him into a taxi?" she queried.

As she asked, Sammy stood up and began to eat the Cheerios that were scattered around his feet. The woman looked at me. "Does this happen often?" she asked. I began to laugh from relief. "No," I assured her, it doesn't. I told the nurse we seemed to be okay as Sammy resumed his walk as if nothing happened. I don't know who this kind woman was, it turned out she was in the city visiting her daughter from Oregon to baby sit their grandchildren. But, though she was now late, she walked three blocks with me to make sure we were okay. There is a lot to be said for the kindness of strangers.

I began to understand that this ear syndrome took many shapes and evolved differently depending on where Sammy was. It has happened about seven times in 13 ½ years and it is different every time. Most recently it came with violent ear flapping, the result of an ear infection which lead to dizziness. The flapping was not only because Sammy's ear was bothering him but because he was losing equilibrium. I thought he was having a stroke. On this occasion, Beatriz was with me in my apartment and as Sammy lashed from side to side I tried to bring him down to the floor for fear he would crack his head into a piece of furniture. He did not get down easily and it took two us to hold him, while I once again called the vet frantic and screaming that my dog was stroking.

The vet, who I guess no longer viewed me as a revenue churner, was not helpful, telling me that they were not an on-call service. It was a rude awakening. After a combined total of over twenty five years as a client, I expected more. I received a somewhat apologetic call that afternoon, explaining that there had been multiple emergencies going on that morning, but still . . . .

Sandra came over later that day, first hearing about what happened when I texted her. She cleaned out Sammy's ears. They were filthy. I could not believe what was coming out. Always prepared, Sandra had brought swabs and slides and captured some of the horrific black gook, so it could be looked at under a microscope. It turned out he had a very bad ear infection, and the cure was to wash his ears daily for ten days and use ear drops.

What would we do without her in our lives???

CHAPTER 31

ANOTHER MOVE? WHEN WILL IT STOP?

One early Sunday evening, Sammy and I were enjoying a short nap in my bedroom when the roar of what sounded like a buzz saw broke through the tranquil calm of the late afternoon. I quite literally flew, almost fell, off the bed. "What the hell?" I wondered out loud and then it came again. It sounded as if someone was trying to drill through my ceiling.

I called my doorman to discover that a new family had moved in above me and had joined two apartments. Their master bedroom was on top of mine. I could not imagine, though a long time New Yorker and used to a lot of bad neighbor behavior, who could possibly think this was okay.

I went upstairs to introduce myself and swore to be "nice," not wanting to assume the worst. I rapped on the door as no one answered the ring of the doorbell. An ominous portent as I knew someone was there. A mid-thirty-ish woman answered and when I expressed my unhappiness with the noise, she asked me to wait while she got the tenant. She was only the decorator, she apologized.

A ramrod straight-backed woman greeted me, hair twisted back off her neck, wearing a tee shirt and jeans. I stretched out my hand and we sized each other up as men often do, with the strength of our grip. I explained that whatever she was doing was extremely intrusive and loud and she said they were trying to hang a flat screen TV in the bedroom. No, "I'm sorry," or "I had no idea you could hear it." No, this woman said, "just hang in there, we'll be done soon." Somewhat incredulous I reminded her it was after 7 on a Sunday evening. She was unfazed. I told her I was going to take my dog out for a walk and expected to return to a quiet bedroom. My upstairs neighbors up until then had been exemplary. Even with a toddler, their carpeted apartment didn't allow much noise through. This new neighbor I realized quickly had taken up all the carpeting and varnished the wood to a high gleam.

When I returned from walking Sammy, the noise had morphed into hammering. Clearly, this was a sadly typical New York neighbor who didn't care about anyone else. My favorite kind!

The next day I complained to the management company and was summarily told that they were paying $9,000 a month in rent and if I didn't like living under them I could move. The superintendent tried to reason with the woman, because she was obviously running the show – "running" being the operative word.

Within the next two weeks it turned out they had a small dog, who was crated in the bedroom and left there to bark for hours, almost six I counted one day, with no abatement. And, then came the husband, at least six foot six inches of him who walked like all of Jurassic Park combined. And, then, not to be outdone by Dad, came Mom's stilettos and the indoor running, stomping and roller skating of the two children who viewed the parquet floors as a roller rink.

With no carpeting to shield the noise, there was never a calm or quiet moment. It became unbearable. I called the managing agent and discovered there were two vacant apartments in the building and both on the side street side. I decided to move into one after learning my new upstairs neighbor was a psychologist who used the apartment as an office and lived elsewhere. What a stroke of luck.

I began my now familiar routine of taking Sammy to visit. Because the new apartment was on our floor, we just had to walk the distance to the other half of the building and we did this daily, several times. The reality was this new apartment was directly across from my old one and I had secretly admired its layout for several years. Now I was going to get to live in it. It was very strange to look out the window and see a reverse of the view I had been used to. Sammy was confused. Now almost 11 years old, he didn't really want to move. Yes, he enjoyed exploring, but that's where it ended.

Nevertheless, move we did. As in previous moves, I had the apartment painted and then we visited. I had carpeting installed. We visited, slowly bits of my old apartment materialized in the new space; light fixtures, drapery and finally everything else. Sammy didn't know where to go. The directions of the layout confused him. I would find him heading out of the bedroom into the bathroom. The only saving grace was with older age, he was losing some of the upper level hearing that used to unnerve him so terribly. Now, the sounds of motorcycles and even thunder were becoming less troublesome. Ha, I thought, a good outcome of aging. Who knew??

CHAPTER 32

A LITTLE SAMMY MUSIC

My sweet dog has a repertoire of sounds that make me happy. I will miss them so dearly when he is no longer with me. Most of all I love the sound of his snoring. It lulls me to sleep.

Sammy has a variety of snores, but the one I love best starts softly and continues like a deep breath. It trails through several octaves, gently moving him along as he sleeps. Rhythmical and loose, they carry him towards a dream. When he reaches this destination, his snore may morph into a soft dream bark that is muted, but distinct. When, on rare occasion, the bark sounds more like a cry, I call to him to pull him out of the badland he has wandered into, although this may be more in my mind than in his.

Along with Sammy's dream snores, he has movement; not just ordinary doggy asleep fluttering of eyelids and flapping of paws, Sammy dreams as if he is possessed. His legs flail in the air as he thrashes. He seems about to levitate when he pauses, takes a few deep breaths and enters Phase two of REM sleep. Sometimes, it looks to me as if he is back in the park kicking fall leaves in every direction, spinning and turning in mounds of red, gold and brown dry foliage, dirt from the path, flying everywhere. I hope he's there because we can't go to the park anymore due to age, but maybe he can visit in his sleep.

Sammy's breathing during the night calms me as well. Depending on whether or not he has mashed his nose into a corner of his round bed, his breathing either has a normal in and out cadence or sounds like soft, swooshing noises. There seems, in older age, to be comfort in burying his nose deep into the faux suede of the bolster that surrounds the bed. It has an orthopedic foam cushion designed for older joints and he can sleep seven hour stretches in its embrace. I never tire or fail to take note of his sounds.

Among the sounds I can't interpret are grunts and grumbles that I have learned can mean, "I am not comfortable," "I want water," and "Please shut up. You're talking too much." This grumble frequently occurs when I try to speak to a friend on the phone, dial my phone or watch television.

His sounds form a distinct pattern in my life and I am always tuned in.

CHAPTER 33

OLDER AND WISER

Aging doesn't happen from one day to the next and yes I had noticed that Sammy's hearing and vision weren't as keen as before, but old??? Not my dog!

I was appalled when people began, slowly at first, to make comments; "*Oh, he's getting up there, huh?*" or "*He's an old guy, huh?*" or my favorite, "*He's old isn't he? How old is he?*" In the beginning I bristled. "He's not old," I would respond. But truth be told he was 11. Was he old? No. In every way that mattered he was still his same old Sammy self; rambunctious, stubborn, willful, playful, handsome. Still Sammy!!!!

Our walking behavior didn't change, but the people we encountered on our walks did. It was quite remarkable to hear people walking around me, talking to one another and saying "*Ah, look at the old guy.*" My dog walkers were equally indignant. Had we all missed something we wondered to one another. But, slowly I saw differences. Instead of flipping over on his back in glee, Sammy now went down on one leg and then rolled himself down. Sometimes he tripped. But, he still bounded on and off my bed and in all respects was himself as I had always known him. But, he wasn't.

Jumping on to my bed, which no longer had a frame, to bring it closer to the floor, became a little hit and miss at first and then a lot of miss. But, he wanted to be on my bed. So, I did a trick of the Cheerios to help propel him. We would begin in the foyer and get a Cheerio. Then we move into the bedroom with me acting a cheerleader, clapping him on as he began his leap. Eventually, I needed to get behind him once he was airborne and help him complete the jump. Sometimes we didn't quite make it up and landed on the floor together. At those times he looked at me with a "what's up?" question mark in his eyes.

It was from the bed that I saw a problem developing. His nurse/vet Sandra came to take him out but he was sleeping on my bed. Always in a paroxysm of unadulterated joy at the sight of her, he flew off the bed and a tiny trickle of liquid spilled out from under him.

"Oh my God," I panicked and look at Sandra. "Did he just pee?"

"Nah, I don't think so. I think it's what we call schmegma, a discharge of residual gunk from the sheathing around his penis."

Schmegma, I pondered. A good Yiddish word and I was fine to leave it at that, but wasn't completely convinced, Something new to watch for.

I became more hyper vigilant than usual, which is to say a bit more neurotic than average. I noticed that on the street I was more aware of the clippety, clippety sound of his nails on the pavement. It seemed at times he was dragging his feet a bit. Was this in my head? He didn't lift his leg quite as high as before when urinating. I logged every nuance into my mental Sammy notebook. It seemed the pages were getting fuller.

Everything happened slowly. I felt as if I was watching my mother go from older to old again. I didn't accept most of what I saw, but kept drawing parallels to my mother often enough. It seems I have some issues about accepting the aging process in those I love until they smack me in the face.

With my mother it was the first time I saw her without her dentures and her little blonde wig, dressed in a lightweight nightgown, so all her bony angles jutted out to smack me in the face. When had this transformation taken place? Like Sammy, who didn't have black fur around his mouth, I didn't get to see the greying. When my mother was stripped of all the outer trappings that made her look so elegant even in her 90's, there was a fragile, tiny little old woman. My mother.

And now there was Sammy. Instead of random strangers stopping to guess his breed and comment on his spectacular looks, there was a Greek chorus of age-guessing. He is still beautiful I would defend him inside my head. Look at how beautiful he is. But the chorus of admiration was dwindling.

I tried acupuncture. Sammy, stoically panted through every session. Was there improvement? Not so much. I was hoping for an elixir of youth. It wasn't at the end of the tiny needles. Now 12 years old, I thought he was doing pretty well for a big dog. I started asking other dog owners the age of their companions and then I would compare. "Well, Sammy can still do this and he does that better." I soothed myself into some sort of comfort zone.

We ran into Ellen and Mugsy one day. Mugs is a year older than Sammy and about 25 pounds lighter and so full of her old high-powered self. Unlike Sammy, she had recurring issues with her teeth, a tumor had developed above one and had to be removed. Another comparison I made. I invited them up to see our new apartment and once inside Mugsy ran amuck as always, flying and barking from one room to the other. But, Sammy couldn't keep up. He looked at me. "What was happening?" we both seemed to be wondering. "When had this happened?" He lay down and Mugsy danced and barked around him. He smiled as he always did around his first love, but he couldn't join in. My heart hurt. They left because I could see his frustration building.

One of the saddest aspects of Sammy aging and it might have happened even if he had been younger, was that he was always a vigorous tail wagger. His tail would thump, thump, thump and drum against walls, cupboards, furniture and especially against the angled corner of the kitchen in our previous apartment. He would wait for his meals and thwack his tail in anticipation of food to the point that I would chide him and say "you're going to break your tail one of these days."

My vet upon examining his defeated tail told me it wasn't broken when I realized he wasn't wagging as strongly as before and there seemed to be a thickening around it towards the base of his rump. She explained it might be inflamed but was anatomically sound. But, his tail began to droop and so did my heart. My heartache was growing. So many changes. I realized that through the years my assumptions about dogs who I saw on the street with curved in tails might not have been the victims of abuse as I had always thought. Their tails might have hurt or they may have been naturally afraid of being outdoors. Sammy's friend Oliver was in this category. I waited for Sammy's tail to heal and the thickening did, indeed, get less and less obvious, but he never really regained the ability to wag it anymore. There was also a possibility it was related to a looming back or hip issue. I worried a lot.

Sammy's older years have been largely defined by his hind legs. Now looking more like rickety kitchen chair legs, they are less sturdy and less reliable. I can still see the willingness to leap in his eyes, but not in his body. It seems to me to be such a failure in the grand scheme of life that old age should be dealt to one in a series of blows and denials. I don't mind my aging as much as I mind Sammy's on his behalf.

CHAPTER 34

OH, MY ACHING BACK

On the subject of backs and legs, I did quite a few rather stupid things in our first year together. One affected my back, and still does.

In an exuberant burst of wild energy and speed, Sammy tore down the hall of my old apartment, our first co-shared domicile, and tripped or sprained or otherwise injured his right hind leg. A lot of limping ensued, but by this point in our relationship I had been given a wonder drug called DeraMaxx. One tablet once a day for one or two days usually left him without pain and noticeable signs of a limp. We were always well stocked.

The problem was when Sammy was thus injured he wanted to do whatever he would normally do and in this case it was jump up on to my bed. He tried, but I stopped him when I saw he didn't stand a chance and went into a squat on his right side. I then wrapped my arms around him like hefting a barrel and proceeded to hoist him off his legs.

Dear God, to go from not being able to carry heavy grocery bags to bench pressing 60 pounds, I had no concept of what this kind of dead weight felt like. But, I was in the middle of the lift and got him on to the bed. And off the bed. And on the bed. Around five times by my estimation, until I didn't like the way my back felt. Had I stopped at one, I might have gotten away with it, but five, not so lucky. The next day my right big toe went numb.

I have to say in many respects I am as willful as my dog. So, without consulting a doctor, I went to an acupuncturist located in a basement storefront as ubiquitous as Korean grocers in Manhattan. The little Chinese woman inserted her set of needles and when she took them out proceeded to perform acupressure, followed by a procedure called cupping, in which hot, glass globes are somehow suctioned to the skin. It hurt and so did my back. So, naturally, I returned for more!

When I realized this wasn't working, I went to an old physical therapy center I had once gone to and self prescribed my therapy. They went along with my diagnosis and when that didn't help I committed the worst mistake of all. I remembered my old dog walker Marco and the chiropractor I had sent him to on the west side of West End Avenue. Marco claimed that this man had cured him of the "Eiiiiiii, pain that stabbed him like a knife." So, off I went.

A stocky, silver haired athletic looking man in his 50's assured me he could fix me. By now my right foot was entirely affected with a numbing, yet stinging pain, my right ankle was on fire and my back made it impossible to sleep. There was no position that worked. So, I handed my back over to this maker of miracles and after three visits, with everything deteriorating rapidly, I asked him, "Are you sure this will work?" I saw uncertainty in his eyes as he said yes. I didn't go back.

But, by now I was dragging my foot behind me as if it was encased in cement. It was Christmas. I had no dog walkers. I cried in pain as I walked Sammy. I sat down on the steps of brownstones and tried to find the stamina to get home. There were no doctors to be had. Everyone was away and in truth I knew no one.

Finally, I called New York's renowned Hospital for Special Surgery and was given an appointment with a pain management physician. I didn't know what the specialty did exactly, but I could barely wait to be seen. The pain had become so intense.

I saw my new doctor on January 2nd and he told me I needed an MRI. It was around the corner on the next block but I couldn't walk. I didn't know how I was going to lay down for the MRI. This kind, new doctor in my life prescribed one 10 mg of Valium to be picked up on the way to the radiologist. I swallowed the pill but it barely nipped at the corner of my pain. I was slid into the MRI tunnel, hands folded on my chest, crying. The technician, whose disembodied voice shared the tunnel with me kept asking if I wanted to stop. I did, desperately, but knew without this diagnosis I was nowhere so I forced my way through it and went back to the doctor. I had a significant herniation between my L5, S1 vertebrae and a facet of one vertebra was pressing on my sciatic nerve. The doctor suggested an epidural injection for the following day. I had no idea what was involved.

The next day found me in a hospital gown, with a blue hair net over my head limping into an operating room. Five people milled around a variety of equipment as my doctor explained what he was going to do, to this assortment of orthopedic fellows, nurses and technicians. I alone didn't quite understand what was about to happen. Finally, it was my turn. He showed me the MRI film and explained that he was going to inject a steroid into the space around the nerve to calm the inflammation. Was it going to hurt? Yes, but he was going to inject a numbing agent first.

It turns out there were to be three layers of injectables. I was asked to lay on the gurney on my stomach, while someone's hands gently pulled my underwear down to the middle of my buttocks. A pillow was under my belly leaving my butt elevated. A beautiful sight I could only imagine. The doctor draped me, swabbed my back and walked me through every step. "You're going to feel a stick," said my doctor. The first needles hurt in an unexpected way. I had never been stuck in this part of my body before. Hrmph, I mumbled. "Are you okay?" he asked. "Uh huh," I said. I couldn't manage more.

"I am going to inject some dye," he told me, "You're going to feel pressure." Yes, he was right. Pressure I did feel, all the way down my right leg. More grunts and mumbles from me, more "are you okays," from him. Then came the actual injection. Wow, was I unprepared for this. The pressure intensified into a pain that I could only liken to a cartoon image of a cat whose tail had been inserted into an electrical outlet. I broke into a sweat, He stopped. "Do you want a minute?" he asked kindly, "I still have half the dose to put in." A nurse held my sweaty hand. "Just squeeze my hand," she told me and I did, for all my life because I knew I needed this.

In recovery afterward I was told what to expect and what to do and not do in the next 48 hours. A little wobbly, I got into a car service car and came home and proceeded to get better. It was amazing. On Day 4, when Sammy came down with what was diagnosed as a form of canine influenza, I was actually able to walk, pain-free to the vet, where he needed to stay for three days.

We both recovered. I am now, eight years later, a veteran of at least 15 epidurals. None have ever been as difficult as the first, but I sometimes wish for that initial pain as it was miraculous in its potency.

Have I stopped lifting Sammy? Not exactly. I just do it differently now. I have never learned how to say no and he has never stopped asking to get his needs met. He is such a grand master in this respect.

CHAPTER 35

FETCH!!!

I have to give Sammy credit. He trained me well, from Day 1. I was obedient and mindful and somehow always understood what he was asking. Our connection has always been remarkable. I can sense him from another room and he senses me.

As he has gotten to 13 more of life's pleasures have been denied to him though I have diligently tried to make up the deficits. Since he can't or doesn't want to chew his rubber Gumby's anymore, I have dutifully lined them up like little green soldiers and he does a doggy drive by in which he knocks them down. I applaud and set them up again and down they come again. It's a different game. No more ripping and tearing. But mischief is never far from his eyes.

His old age is punctuated by what I can only describe as "Don't tell me what to do!" He sends me this message in many small and large ways and always proceeds to do what he wanted to do before I so rudely butt in!

CHAPTER 36

THE WINTER OF OUR DISCONTENT.....
MAKE THAT INCONTINENCE

There are times in our lives that are turning points. We all experience them and Sammy and I reached one around his 13th year. From his early days with me when everything was fair game on which for him to pee, to his many years when he would absolutely never think of raising his leg indoors, we arrived at the point where "accidents" happened. The first was, in retrospect, the time he jumped off my bed and Sandra declared his spill to be schmegma. Looking back I realize it was a trickle of urine that escaped his bladder when he jumped.

Those trickles became more frequent as we approached the winter of 2013 and 2014. In fact, they forced me to place a wee wee pad in front of my bed to catch these involuntary dribbles. I began to read about diapers for dogs. They came in a variety of sizes and colors, but I settled on what are known as belly bands for male dogs, since as Sandra says "their junk is in the front." Turns out female dogs get to wear the little pull up kind, but male dogs need to be treated differently. I found faux, micro-suede belly bands with funny names on the top such as Wiz Claiborne and Tommy Peeflger, but the names weren't amusing me. I was unhappy that

I had to confront this turn of events and decided that the belly bands would be good for Sammy as a means of getting him from the bed to the elevator, as I didn't want him to hang around in a wet diaper. But, it seems we weren't quite at that stage yet. And then came the snow!

The winter months between 2013 and 2014 were brutal in the frequency of snow days. The snow would have been bad all by itself, but in New York City when a doorman is armed with salt or, worse yet, a salt spreader, even getting out of the building can be fraught with pain for dogs. I tried, in vain, to put boots on Sammy, but while he was compliant about having them put on his paws, he refused to walk in them. Beatriz and I tried to figure out how to make an endless variety of waterproof socks for him, but he would have no part of this. Patient as a saint he would watch as we rolled our newest creation on his paws and then in disgust kicked each one off as he walked away.

The situation was comical, but the reality was bad. When an older dog is already having issues with arthritic joints, having to raise a paw as an indication that salt had crawled in between his toes is difficult. From our first winters together I had always walked Sammy with a wad of wet paper towels in a plastic bag in my coat pocket. When he registered pain from salty slush and his paw went up, out came my trusty rescue towel. Relief was quick and we would walk on. But as Sammy aged it seems the pads of his paws were drier and he succumbed more easily to salt. Newer, cheaper varieties were appearing on the street and they were more caustic, not to mention the horrendous salt the city used to blanket the streets. Navigating this was nightmarish.

So, here we were in a winter that was worse than all the others we had experienced at earlier ages. Once entranced and excited with fluffy mounds of the white stuff pouring from the sky, Sammy now approached snow with caution. So did I. But, it kept coming in this dreadful winter. Two inches, ten inches, it seemed there was always snow. One morning we went out to walk and as we came out of the elevator, my dear overnight doorman looked at us in dismay. "I just salted," he said eying Sammy. With that he opened the front door, indicated that I should hold it and he scooped up Sammy in his arms and carried him to the corner where he had not deposited any salt. He waited in the cold until we came back and carried Sammy to the building. Such kindness. I was overwhelmed. I wish everyone else had been as amazing, but not many were.

At 5:30 on a frigid Sunday morning after yet another snowy downpour, we headed out to walk in the early morning darkness. The building next door to mine was five years old and had installed, wonder of wonders, heaters under their sidewalk to melt snow and ice. But, even this otherwise trusty system was having a problem thawing the frozen snow. As we approached 86th street, a large intersection, Sammy pulled to cross over. My gut said no, but he was determined, so we began to cross. As we approached the other side, Sammy held up one paw, then two and then went belly down with salt in all four paws. I whipped out my wet towels but the salt overwhelmed him and I couldn't get him upright. Laying in the cold slush and salt in his winter coat he looked at me helplessly. I began to scream for help. I tried to wave down a taxi and a bus, but no one saw me and worse yet we were still well enough in the street to be hit by a car. Two people walked past me within ten feet of us and I cried to them for help, but they just kept walking. I was stunned.

I tried and tried to lift Sammy up but couldn't. Finally, a woman with a German Shepard began crossing the intersection, and I called out to her. "I will help," she said but continued to walk. I wailed in despair and she turned to me. "Just let me tie my dog to the lamppost," she said and came back to us. With a supreme act of mercy which must have ruined her coat, she helped me carry Sammy, flat as a pancake, back to our corner. I maneuvered him into the building on the corner where two doormen helped me clean his feet well enough for us to get to the next building, home. It was horrific.

And, the winter went on unrelenting. I decided to walk Sammy in the building wearing the belly band, hoping he would empty his bladder out. But though we walked from one floor to another he was not understanding this new concept.

So, before the next storm I had an idea. I would re-create the street for him in the basement of our building. I collected twigs, leaves, fallen tree branches from the street. Anything that looked as if it had been marked by another dog was fair game. Everything went into a plastic garbage bag. I must have looked like a crazed bag lady. I ripped duct tape off scaffolding pillars and eyed the orange plastic mesh used at our electric utility's construction sites. Sammy loved this mesh. But how to cut off a piece, I wondered? My wonderful vet nurse snagged a piece for us. About two feet long it looked perfect.

So, the night of the next storm Lidia, who stayed overnight with me, helped me dress Sammy as if we were going out for a walk on the street. On went the belly band, then his coat, then his leash. I grabbed my garbage bag of street bounty and went ahead of them to create the "street scene."

Sammy walked into the basement and smelled everything with interest, but there was no pee. We walked up and down this make-shift street without any success. Finally, I said to Lidia who was dressed in a coat, "let's open the basement door to the courtyard and see if he can walk." The snow was already past her ankles and blowing hard. Sammy waded into the drifts and as the wind caught his coat I spied the belly band. We had forgotten to take it off!!!!!

He came back indoors and I removed it. It was saturated, but as it turned out, not enough so. The next day, every time he stood up, urine spilled out of him. Sandra came over and watched in disbelief. "I have never seen this before," she exclaimed to my dismay. I told her of the events the night before and we concluded that because he hadn't fully voided his bladder, it had stretched and stretched and was now disgorging its contents. It was the beginning of wall to wall wee wee pads. My beautiful apartment slipped under a swath of extra large white pads bordered in blue and so we live, still!! I can no longer remember what the apartment actually looks like. On top of the wee wee pads are waterproof blankets made specifically for doggy "accidents." I use them to provide some extra padding and comfort for Sammy's bones to rest on. Along with this are plastic bath mats that keep people from slipping in the tub. They line the wooden floors in my apartment to provide a skid-proof surface as he walks from room to room.

CHAPTER 37

LIFE WITH AN OLD DOG

S ammy isn't the only one who is aging. I am too, though not at his rate. Yet the physical nature of what is required to help him is staggering.

I imagine the awful winter contributed to his lack of desire to walk outside. And the more he stayed indoors, the less mobile he became. His interest in life did not decline, but more and more he wanted it brought to him. My bed, once a cozy haven for him, became a challenge of enormous proportions. He would walk to it, eye it mournfully and stand in front of it until I hoisted him up. My bed, during the day, was now also covered in wee wee pads on top of which stretched a sheet. He would get lifted on to the bed plop down uncomfortably. Beatriz and I would turn him in a different position, all the while adjusting his legs and head for comfort. And, so he would drift into sleep. When he woke up, we would help him down and he went to the next stop on the Sammy route of the day.

He was walking outdoors, slowly, but walking nonetheless. Yet, he looked so old. He performed his Sammy swirling pees, accomplished without lifting his leg. His pees looked like signature graffiti. I have never seen another dog do this. His swirls could stretch over 5-10 feet. He still stopped to chat with doormen and still tried to find poop. In all ways, his old self, but modified and slow.

It occurred me one day that he didn't like wearing his collar anymore. I never kept it on him at home, but now it seemed to bother him on his walks. I tried a new harness and finally, Beatriz and I concocted a loop mechanism to attach to his coat to which we clicked on his leash. Better yes. Control, not so much. The leash would pull his coat this way and that as Sammy pulled this way and that. Walking him became difficult for me. My back wasn't up to the task. What would we do when the weather turned warm, I wondered, and there was no coat to which to attach the leash.

I was struck over and over by how stealthily old age had crept up on him. It stole tiny bits of routines, small chunks of pleasure, but so discreetly that by the time it was noticeable it was overwhelmingly sad. My otherwise healthy dog was having life slowly sapped away.

In the summer of 2014 Beatriz's husband suffered a massive heart attack and for a few days it was touch and go. Lidia and a cousin of Beatriz', Andrea, who had helped with Sammy when he was 12, filled in the void left by her need to be with her husband, first in the hospital and then at home.

The first morning that Andrea appeared instead of Beatriz I heard her come in and then heard Sammy bark. Not an ordinary bark, it sounded like "Get out, get out." It was loud and unfriendly. Andrea who knew Sammy as an affectionate and welcoming soul was scared. I heard her saying over and over "Sammy, it's me." But, I finally had to intercede. He wanted no part of her and she was so surprised at how old he had become. She was afraid to try to walk him and he had no interest in going out with her. So, in the seven weeks of Beatriz' absence, Sammy stopped walking in the morning. We had given up his 5:30 in the morning walks several months prior as he simply slept through the time.

My weekly wee wee pad bill was huge, but I needed to accommodate him and still maintain a clean, albeit odd looking, apartment.

I had bought little wooden tables made to help dogs eat by not stretching their necks down too far. There were three; one for water, one for food and one for snacks in my bedroom. His wonderful, cozy round bed with its orthopedic mattress was covered with a wee wee pad and a sheet and changed whenever he got out of it. I watched as he began to hug the wall for balance occasionally and was struck so often by how much his aging resembled my mother's. Aging, it seems, is pretty much an equal opportunity condition.

So, here life finds us approaching Sammy's 14th birthday. Where Sammy used to leap to embrace life, now it pretty much has to be brought to him.

He walks outside rarely these days, but is, in most respects, a healthy oldster. If Sammy was a human he would have an aide and walker, the deluxe kind, of course. His appetite is strong and vigorous and he loves to "mingle and dingle," as Lidia says, with anyone who comes to the apartment. Mostly, I have noticed his "mingling and dingling" has everything to do with treats. When there are none he loses interest quickly. In fact, when there are no more "crummies" left, he begins this low "grrrr." I have figured out that it is the official Sammy dismissal. "You got nothing more for me," he seems to say, "then may I suggest you get out." It is so rude, but so Sammy.

Sandra gets him outdoors periodically for very encapsulated walks during which she crab walks behind him with one hand on each of his haunches. She isn't carrying him, rather preventing him from falling back when he pauses mid-walk, struck by a particularly interesting spot of pee or, if the gods are merciful, a tantalizing piece of poop that he is no longer swift enough to snag.

Recently, Sandra showed up one evening looking very serious. "I have some news," she said not making eye contact. I was scared.

Either something was wrong with Sammy that I wasn't aware of or she was quitting. But, no. As she told me, she showed up for work at the veterinary clinic three days prior to find that a woman posturing herself as a "neighbor" of mine, had called to complain to Sandra about Sandra, who had the day off. She asked for my vet. How she knew where Sandra works, or what her name is, much less the clinic with which she is affiliated takes me into "stalker" territory and not a good place to think about.

Nonetheless, the "neighbor's" complaint was that Sandra and my vet were not taking good care of this "poor, suffering animal," and she was upset that he wasn't being put to sleep. She managed to get my vet on the phone to vent these complaints along with how skinny Sammy was and that he wasn't eating.

Now, in fairness, anyone seeing Sandra do her crab walk with my dog would not likely understand what was going on. But, in fact, I needed him to walk to get gravity working on organs like his bladder. He needed to move, never in pain or against his will, but to get his body to remember how to work more efficiently. I am blessed that Sandra is even willing or able to do this.

Anyone with arthritis can attest to the fact that movement is critical for stiff joints. But, how this so called neighbor of mine could call Sammy "skinny," is beyond everyone. He eats like the three little pigs on steroids and probably a little weight loss would be a good idea, but eating is one of his pleasures. How could this stranger divine what was going on in the confines of my home??? We puzzled about this and discovered individual recollections of a woman in her 60's, who seems to appear on the 85th street side of my building and knows my dog by name. She has run into Beatriz, Natalia and even behind Sandra, who could not see her because she was focused on Sammy. It does not seem that she actually lives in my building. Not truly a neighbor. This is New York, and as insular as it can be, it is also fair game for just about anything and in this case it is disturbing.

We can only surmise that she saw Sandra, wearing her scrubs, on the night she walked Sammy. Assuming she was a medical person of some sort, she must have waited for Sandra to leave my building and then followed her back to the veterinary clinic. How she knew her name will remain a mystery. How she dared to fabricate parts of her story is appalling.

I revealed this story to a neighbor of mine who has an Airedale terrier and has lived through several old dogs. She was appalled but looked thoughtful and said "I bet I know who it might have been," she confided. There were two suspects that immediately came to mind for her. I knew them both but was stunned by the idea that either could have fabricated this story, made up pieces and followed Sandra, for clearly that's what someone did.

I understand that seeing a once vigorous dog become old and look a bit paraplegic can be disconcerting. But quality of life is based on a lot of factors and I examine all of these frequently. I look into Sammy's eyes for answers and still see a blazing spirit. The cock of his ears still picks up the sounds that tell him all is right with his world and while his vision and hearing are not as they were in his youth, they still work.

I wasn't much of a physical help for my mother in her last years. She required more strength and, truthfully, more patience, than I had to give. I loved her dearly, but in old age she was very difficult. I am not comparing Sammy to my mother, though would it be so terrible if I did? Old age for each of them confounded me and with Sammy, still confounds me. But, I like to believe in second chances and I am trying to get it right with my dog. So I stretch, bend, look like I am playing Twister when I am home with him. He frustrates me with his lack of cooperation most of the time and then I imagine my life without him and switch gears. Sammy is still with me. I am blessed.

CHAPTER 38

QUESTIONS MARKS

Nevertheless, almost every day now the swarm of question marks swirls around my head and my heart like mosquitos. And, I am not the only one asking. Natalia hearing Sammy grousing, asks me "What does he want, do you know?" Lidia frequently remarks that I always know what he wants, but in truth, I do not and I am frustrated.

I have had conversations with my vet and Sandra about end of life scenarios and they are awful. Extinguish a life? Such a terrible responsibility. Yet, everyone concurs, and I can see, that my dog is very much among the living.

Sammy was entrusted to my care. However this came about and whether or not he truly embodies the spirit of my cat, Astor, which I have long suspected, will have to remain one of life's mysteries. I only hope I am wise enough to recognize when he no longer wants to participate. But, that time isn't upon us yet.

I check his blood and urine every three months to ensure that nothing is brewing and Sandra clips his nails which aren't being naturally ground down by walking on hard NYC concrete. He sleeps longer and wants what he wants, when he wants it. In that respect, nothing is new. I trust Sammy will give me the cue I need to understand my next steps or he will drift away with the knowledge that he has been so incredibly loved and appreciated for his innate "Sammy-ness." For the moment we're still here.

Sadly, Beatriz felt a hard lump on her dog, Mike's belly a few weeks ago. Labs are prone to developing large, fatty cysts, but this wasn't one of them. I metabolized her fear. It became mine. Mike's legs, at 12 ½ had been wobbly for almost a year and with Alberto's surgery still a fresh reality, it was difficult to get Mike into their car. So, the vet came to their home. He felt the lump and looked grave, drew blood and urine and the next day pretty much confirmed that he believed it was liver cancer.   Did he know for sure without a biopsy? No. Were Alberto and Beatriz willing to put Mike through a battery of tests? No.

Everyone knew the truth because it was in Mike's eyes. He looked sad and uncomfortable. His breathing was labored and the decision was made. Beatriz came to work on Monday and Mike's euthanasia was scheduled for Tuesday morning. I couldn't bear her pain because there was nothing to say, other than the platitude that we can do more for our animals than we can for human suffering. It is a gift that she can end his pain I tell her along with everyone else who knows and loves Mike.

In absolutely every sense a cherished animal's death is every bit as potent and terrible as human death. It leaves behind a crater of emptiness that nothing can fill. I remember my grief and pain when I released Abbie. I remember saying "never again." The years evaporate amidst fresh mourning for a dog, not my own. I am more fearful than before, understanding once again how short life is and how easily it succumbs to finality.

CHAPTER 39

IS ANYONE OUT THERE?

I spoke to a psychic after Abbie died. My hair colorist, Chuck, responding to my pain, told me of a "sensitive" who lives outside of London. I had to speak to her he insisted. The transaction, in American currency, preceding the telephone conversation, is required before you get to speak and when this lilting British voice came on line I hoped she would immediately tell me that she was speaking to Abbie. But, no. She rambled on about this and that until I lost patience. I didn't care about anything she was telling me.

"Do you see spirits?" I finally asked. I knew I was feeding her, but I could have been asking about a deceased spouse, parent, or friend. It was startling when she said "Of course I do and it's funny that you ask, because since we've been speaking there has been a cat curling around my ankles. Have you recently lost a cat?" She asked this so matter of factly. I was startled.

Before I could answer or make any sort of sound, she said, "Wait a moment," she paused. "There are more. I see two more cats. No, make that three, does that make sense?" I was about to say something, when she said, "No, wait a moment, the third cat is actually a small dog. Three cats and a small dog," she proclaimed.

I was speechless. I will never know what to make of this. How did she know? Mister died when I was 20. How could she have known? Even if Chuck had fed her information about Abbie out of kindness and to relieve my pain, he never knew about my childhood dog. There was no earthly way for her to divine this.

There are so many mysteries. This one brings me great comfort and I share it with anyone I know who has suffered loss. We mortals know so little and while I am not religious, I will never understand how this sensitive, named Dorothy, so accurately pinpointed the cast of animals who have enriched my life.

CHAPTER 40

PRE-MOURNING

I walk familiar streets without Sammy, though he is waiting for me at home. I look with great sadness at the places we used to walk together and grief overcomes me in waves. Each part of every street in our neighborhood holds a memory. They are poignant and melancholic. I walk by the church on the corner of 87th street and remember, as Sammy raised his leg, the voice of a woman behind me saying "It's not nice to make pee pee on a church." With a lovely French accent, she walked beside me and I told her I hoped God wouldn't mind too much, but in fact Sammy's leg didn't raise too high anymore and the ground was largely the recipient of whatever watering he was doing.

I pass doormen who ask where Sammy is, how he is, is he at all?? I miss being on the end of his leash, trailblazing the upper west side, seeing it through his eyes.

My dear friend Rachel, a psychotherapist, tells me I am pre-mourning. It feels like that. So much of what I shared with Sammy was now denied to both of us. We would never take these walks again I knew and my heart broke.

CHAPTER 41

THREE IMPERATIVES

Life seemed to go into hyper-drive for me. I had three things I needed to accomplish, quickly. I needed to get the photograph of Sammy on the path by the Delaware river framed and hanged. I needed to finish his story and most of all I wanted to get him to his fourteenth birthday.

I felt time slipping away. It wasn't that Sammy was sick. His appetite was as strong as always and he still loved getting his treats from everyone. He had a visitor almost every night and looked forward to it, but most of the time there was a rolled up towel propping him up as he was getting too weak to lean fully forward.

I got the picture framed and it hangs on the wall where Sammy's water dish used to be. These days water is brought to him. I ask Sandra every day, "How will I know? Is it time?" She says no. She tells me I will know.

CHAPTER 42

HAPPY BIRTHDAY TO SAMMY

You were born on November 28, 2000. Today is your 14th birthday.

Of your 14 years, it took me five to find you and in the nine to follow, I have had the privilege to know you and love you. A cherished friend, we have had our differences along the way, but I have always known that you love me. I hope you always know how much I love you.

Love isn't easy and old age tests even the strongest bonds. Cooperative, you are not, willful and opinionated you are. You sleep longer these days and wake with more difficulty, coming back into this life for another day, one day at a time.

You somehow manage to tame my question marks, even while creating them. You will have the final say, of that I am sure, the answer to the question that is so hard for me to consider. But, Sammy, I will always do what's right for you and trust that you will guide me.

Beloved companion, your life has been a great and mighty gift and as I celebrate your 14 years, I give thanks to all the people who have crossed our path in friendship and love. It has been and will continue to be an extraordinary journey.

CHAPTER 43

FIVE DAYS

My goal was to finish writing Sammy's story by his 14th birthday and I did. At least I thought I did. I stopped writing. But in the five days that followed his birthday, something was beginning to go wrong. The urine that spurted from Sammy often came in a huge gush and I needed to move him quickly to prevent it from covering his legs. While he slept urine pooled under him, saturating the wee wee pad he slept on, and the pristine pink skin around his groin began to develop angry red spots. Sandra advised me to use a topical cream, but it wasn't enough. He couldn't heal fast enough and I was afraid the spots would turn into open sores.

I noticed that he seemed to flinch when he drank water. Sandra had always joked that Sammy had inherited the "good teeth gene," but I fretted that one of his front teeth had become sensitive to water, even though it wasn't cold.

I began to feel desperation crawl inside me and take hold. I couldn't keep up with everything that was breaking down. He suddenly looked so old and frail. My heart began to hurt, tears never far from my eyes. And, then came the pain. It seemed as if out of nowhere.

I noticed Sammy was curling into a U shape as if trying to bring his nose to his tail. I panicked. Sandra had given me a "just in case" painkiller a year before; a liquid in a plastic syringe. I had eight of them. Natalia came in as I my distress was mounting. I had tried to soothe him, but for the first time in his life with me, Sammy snapped at the air in front of my fingers. I understood he needed help quickly. I called Sandra to find out how to deliver the pain medication and with her guidance, Natalia and I managed to plunge the liquid from the syringe into the space between Sammy's upper lip and his cheek. We moved him cautiously into the bedroom, where he lay on the floor as we could see the medicine overtake the pain. He fell asleep. Natalia and I exchanged a look and she left, kissing him on his soft head.

I gently lifted him into his bed and he slept through the night. The next day he seemed better. I was trying to keep my hysteria at bay. But he had rallied. I went to work.

When I came home that evening Lidia was in the living room, with Sammy, waiting for me. "How is he?" I asked. She told me he seemed to be curling up again. I went to get his food and he ate and I had hope, but it was dashed after Lidia left and the curling into a horseshoe began to happen again. I was frantic. I knew what I needed to do. He was telling me.

I called Sandra, It was 7:30. "Sammy is in terrible pain," I told her amidst flowing tears. "What do you want to do?" she asked. "I want it to stop," I said in between sobs. I had already given him another syringe and he seemed to quiet down. Sandra asked, "When?" I said "Now." We both understood. She told me to hang on and she would come as soon as she could get everything together.

Sammy lay asleep on the living room floor and I sat on a dining room chair just watching him, trying not to disturb him. I had once asked Sandra how I would know the time had arrived and she told me "You will be waiting for us at the front door." I was. But, it was happening too fast.

At 9:30 Sandra arrived with a vet I had never met, but of whom Sandra had spoken highly. Sammy was stirring when they walked in. The painkiller had only lasted two hours and he seemed drugged and unfocused. When he saw Sandra he cried out four times. She dropped to her knees consoling him. "It's okay baby, it's okay. We're going to help make it stop." I realized that upon seeing her Sammy reflexively was barking for treats and it was coming out as cries. I handed her a piece of cookie and in his drug stupor he tried to eat it.

The doctor sat behind him. No one questioned where the pain was coming from. It didn't matter. It had arrived. Everyone looked at me. "Please help him," I said. "Make the pain stop." The doctor gave him a shot in his thigh and he flinched, but stilled. I could see him relax. We all changed places as if we had rehearsed this. The vet moved to the front of his left side where his face rested on his paw. Sandra moved to his right front leg and I went behind him, laid down and wrapped him in this one last embrace. The vet quietly said to me, "He can't really move now, but he can hear you." Through my sobs I told my precious dog how much I loved him. I thanked him for being in my life over and over. I held him and stroked him and Sandra inserted an IV line into his front leg. He never registered any discomfort. This was so different than when I had put Abbie to sleep.

The line was in place and an orange liquid was waiting to be injected. I cradled my dog and sobbed giving assent to the process that would stop his heart. Sandra gripped my right hand and I heard her sobbing too. I held him, kissing him and just holding on. Minutes passed. "When will it be over?" I managed to ask the vet. "It has been for a few minutes already," she said softly. I never felt him leave. It was so peaceful. His chin remained on his paw. His pain was over and I felt my life was too.

Sandra tenderly wrapped my dog into his favorite coral fleece blanket and I could feel that his spirit wasn't with me any longer. She and the vet would take him back to the clinic until I could make arrangements. Our life together was over. I went utterly numb.

As Sandra and the vet left with Sammy in Sandra's strong arms, I mutely went around my apartment picking up wee wee pads and blankets and plastic mats. I filled garbage bag after garbage bag and silently walked them out to the garbage pick-up area. It was soon filled with eight large bags. I did this because I didn't want Beatriz to have to do it the next day. I left his toys and his bed untouched.

After I had called Sandra, I had called Beatriz to tell her what I was about to do. She wailed. Inconsolable. Two dogs in two weeks, it was more than anyone should have to bear. She couldn't speak, her sobs were so all consuming. I gently put the receiver back on the cradle. In the morning she would find large 8" by 10" black and white photos of Sammy attached to every surface that corresponded to the part of the apartment in which the photo was taken. I had transferred them from my phone to my printer and taped them all over the apartment. When she came the next morning we hugged each other for a long time and wept. The loss was so total. I couldn't stop crying and neither could she.

My home was still. The quiet was unbearable. I went to work, but told no one what had happened. I was too raw and beyond consolation. My second in command in the office, a lovely, compassionate and empathetic young woman divined that something was wrong. She texted me that evening. "Tell me," she said. "I know something is wrong." I told her, but asked her not to tell anyone else. It would be a month before I could summon up the words and strength.

I did tell my friends, Sammy's Godparents, Steve and Paula, Natalia, Lidia and Harriet, the lady who had delivered Sammy to me nine years earlier. I asked if she needed some coats for future rescues. Our emails were so dear. She understood my loss all too well. She told me she wished every rescue could have a mom like me, but it didn't help.

My home soon filled with roses in every color and size. My lawyer sent me roses and orchids and told me the only time he had ever seen his father cry was when their dog died. He choked up on the phone.

In my heart I never for one moment questioned the action I had taken. My dog died what we humans call "a good death." He was surrounded and bathed in love in the comfort of his home. He simply slipped away with grace and dignity and it felt right. But the loss was so awful. The apartment was quiet and stilled. Sammy had taken up so much of it just by breathing. Without him, it felt unfamiliar and not at all like home. Three months later it still feels like the place I live, but no longer like home. There were no more question marks hanging over me.

EPILOGUE

CHAPTER 1

In spite of my valiant attempts to avoid this awful pain, here I was again. The emptiness of my apartment engulfed me every time I came in and upon waking up in the morning. The absolute nature of the quiet was unsettling.

I believe everyone mourns in their own way. I was blessed to be enfolded in the love of my friends and Beatriz. They all let me cry and sob. I dreaded getting into my elevator for fear a neighbor would ask about Sammy. It happened twice. In the enclosed space of the elevator there was no escape. One neighbor put her hand on my arm and when she started to speak I asked her not to. Another, the lady with the Airedale Terrier, simply enfolded me in an embrace. My doormen looked at me sympathetically. It was so hard. I ran into a couple from my building in a local market and they began to say they knew about Sammy. I held up my hand and turned away. My eyes burned from the constant, unrelenting sting of tears.

Natalia asked me to join her and her husband for dinner. I welcomed this time away from my apartment. An artist, who draws wonderful portraits of dogs, Natalia silently handed me a large white package after dessert. My heart lurched. I knew what was inside and didn't want to cry in the restaurant, but I saw how much they wanted me to open it. Inside was an almost life sized portrait of Sammy. It was an interesting view to have captured. In it, Sammy is seen from the neck up and one ear is pointing straight up in the air. He is lying down and looking out from the picture with an expression I knew very well. It was his *"What?"* expression. *"What do you want?"* it said. Tears overflowed and I had to wrap it up quickly. I barely managed to squeak out a thank you.

The picture was framed within a week and it hangs on the wall above Sammy's toys, which are still where they were left three months ago. A curious thing happened though. As I stared at the framed drawing I noticed, in typical Sammy fashion, the spots behind his neck had formed a face, a puppy version of Sammy. It was as if it was getting ready to make an appearance. I asked Natalia if she did this on purpose and she said no and came over to see it. We found another small dog peering out from under his jaw.

CHAPTER 2

I needed to get Sammy buried and turned, as in previous years, to Abbingdon Hill, to bring my sweet boy back to my other animals. I called my best friend Anne and asked her if she would drive me. I called Beatriz and asked her if she wanted to come. Both said yes.

The cemetery called me when the wooden casket I ordered arrived and we made plans a week after he died to bury him. We made a lot of small talk on the way there. Anne tried to bolster me up and distract me, but I knew what lay ahead and was actually comforted with the thought of seeing Sammy one last time.

When we arrived there was a little snow on the ground and I blinked several times before I could make out a big white cat in front of the building that served as an office for the cemetery. She looked like a mound of snow. As I approached her she nuzzled my hand and went to the door as if this was pre-arranged. Inside was another cat, peacefully snoozing in front of a pot belly stove. I already knew this routine well and when the cemetery keeper led me down the hall to an open door, I knew I would find Sammy in the casket with the lid up. While this may sound morbid, it wasn't. It was an opportunity to say one last goodbye. I put my arm around

Anne and told her it wasn't necessary for her to come in if she didn't want to.

The sight of Sammy, so peaceful and looking as he had so many times over the years, as if he was asleep, made me smile. I walked over and kissed him. He was so cold to the touch, but it didn't matter. Beatriz bent over and coo-ed to him as she had in life. She scratched behind his ears. She needed this closure. This one last caress.

I turned to find Anne behind me, eyes brimming with tears. She hugged me close as she had when my mother died. Sammy was wrapped in the coral fleece blanket and a toy I had sent along was under his arm – a toy Beatriz had given him. I slipped another in as well.

These token gestures we do are for the living. The soul of my dog was no longer present. I couldn't feel him, but I still had the spot I had first smelled and kissed nine years ago and I bent to kiss it again. My tears flowed now and I held Beatriz as she gently sobbed beside me. I asked her if she wanted time alone with him and she did. So Anne and I walked out and I heard her softly speaking to him in Spanish.

We all have to find the peace we need in these moments in our own ways. When my mother died, the funeral home asked me to identify her in the casket and I couldn't. My cousin did. But, with Sammy I stood and stroked his beautiful head, grateful I could do this one more time.

We walked outside to the gravesite and again I was struck by the serenity of this place. Beatriz had brought flowers and I laid some Baby's Breath by Sebastian, because in life he loved to chew on this flower.

I laid roses at the graves of Abbie and Astor and then walked slowly to the open grave into which Sammy's casket had been lowered. Beatriz dropped the roses she brought on top and the undertaker handed me the shovel. I shoveled fresh earth on my beloved dog and completed the act of bringing him back to nature. I feel at peace knowing where his body is. I only wished I knew where his soul has gone. Had he walked down the dusty, red clay trail and met my mother? I wanted a sign.

CHAPTER 3

My lack of routine in the first few weeks was jarring. Without Sammy, I didn't quite know what to do with myself. But life has a way of nudging us forward regardless of where we get stuck. I mourned so deeply with tears routinely spilling down my face. They were so knee-jerk and instantaneous that I had no control. I cried everywhere and with everyone. No one recoiled from my grief. Everyone allowed it and still do. Sometimes in the beginning I could speak about Sammy for a moment, but then the catch in my throat would turn into a sob. It still happens. My grief stays fresh and raw. But, I feel him moving slowly into the distance. That makes me sad, but I understand it has to happen.

I read an article about grief in the New York Times. It spoke to me. It gave me permission to not have control; to not accept the notion that there are steps to the process of grieving. There are no time limits. It talked about "telling the story" of the loss and I felt comforted, because telling Sammy's story felt like a necessity.

So much has happened in the weeks, almost 15 now, that have passed. Unlike almost everyone who has spoken to me about losing an animal, I have never had the experience of feeling that I just saw my dog, or that he was behind me. When Sammy died, he left. But there are things I cannot explain.

Two weeks after he died, on a Sunday, I was reading the newspaper over a cup of coffee in the dining room. A sound, sort of a thunk, made me look up. I kept reading. Another thunk. I couldn't imagine what would make that sort of sound, but it seemed to be coming from my bedroom. It was a sunny day and as often happened, there were streaks of white sunshine on my carpet. But, as if drawn by the sound, I was now drawn by the sight of an ultraviolet-colored ray of light dissecting the floor where Sammy's bed had been. It stretched across my bedroom as I looked at it in astonishment. It came to my feet. I went to the window, which faces another building, taller than mine, to look for the source of what surely was filtering the sunlight. But there was nothing; nothing hanging in a neighbor's window, nothing on top of a building. Nothing at all. The light was beautiful and for two weeks I saw it frequently, always in the same place. Sometimes there were two streaks. I would like to think it was Sammy riding a sunbeam, but my mind is more practical. Yet it was strange.

Stranger was the imprint of Sammy on the floor under where his bed used to be. His bed was made of a four inch thick layer of corrugated foam, on top of which were a wee wee pad and a sheet. His body heat could not have seared his image into the carpet, yet there it was, even including his big black heart. I was mesmerized. How could this have happened? I showed it to Beatriz; took pictures of it and the light. Beatriz has since, wisely, vacuum-cleaned the area over and over and now the imprint is gone. But I have a picture of it. I so desperately want to know that he is somewhere, in some form, that he remembers me, that he still loves me.

CHAPTER 4

Everyone asks me if I will ever do this again? Will I ever have another dog or cat? I was adamant in the beginning when I said no. Even if a Sammy look-alike were to appear out of nowhere, I said, the answer was no. He would not be Sammy.

A friend asked if I would baby sit her 10 year old Silky Terrier, who I knew very well before she moved to London six years ago. I agreed, thinking it would soothe my tattered heart. This adorable, 18 pound dog, named Bear, played with Sammy's toys. I was happy that they made him happy. Sammy always loved to share his toys. I walked with Bear and he slept beside me at night. But, my heart did not open. It was too soon. What did I expect, my friends asked. In the end, it made me more sad. One cannot replace one being with another. It does not mean one cannot move on.

I love watching dogs on the street and pet some when I can. Not all are open to this. I made arrangements for Sammy's headstone. It will read:

My Sweet
Sammy
Beloved and Cherished Companion

Harriet has been in touch with me. Would I consider fostering a dog? I say no. But, I don't say "Never again."

⇥⇤

ABOUT THE AUTHOR

 Suzanne Lane owns a successful public relations agency in New York City. She chose to write the story of her relationship with Sammy in order to share her experiences with other dog lovers and potential animal rescuers. She mostly wanted to memorialize an extraordinary dog who changed her life.

Made in the USA
Middletown, DE
10 July 2017